*Better Handwriting in 30 Days*

# Better Handwriting
## in 30 Days

*Developing a More Attractive,*
*Readable Script for Business,*
*School, and Personal Satisfaction*

Paula A. Sassi

JEREMY P. TARCHER, INC.
Los Angeles

Picasso, Salk, O'Neill, and Twain writing samples from "The Book of Autographs," copyright © 1978 by Book Creations, Inc. Reprinted by permission of Book Creations, Inc.

D'Nealian® alphabet from *D'Nealian® Handwriting* by Donald Thurber. Copyright © 1987 by Scott, Foresman and Company. Reprinted by permission.

Excerpts and illustration from *Drawing on the Right Side of the Brain* by Betty Edwards. Copyright © 1979 by Betty Edwards.

Excerpt and illustration from *Whole-Brain Thinking* by Jacquelyn Wonder and Priscilla Donovan. Illustration by Wayne Salge. Copyright © 1984 by Jacquelyn Wonder and Priscilla Donovan. Used by permission of William Morrow and Company, Inc.

Library of Congress Cataloging in Publication Data


Sassi, Paula A.
  Better handwriting in 30 days: developing a more attractive,
readable script for business, school, and personal satisfaction /
Paula A. Sassi.
      p. cm.
    Bibliography.
    1. Penmanship. I. Title.
  Z43.S277 1989
  652'.1—dc19
    ISBN 0-87477-510-8                                    89-30587
                                                          CIP

Jeremy P. Tarcher, Inc.
9110 Sunset Blvd.
Los Angeles, CA 90069

Distributed by St. Martin's Press, New York

*Design by Robert Tinnon*

Manufactured in the United States of America
10 9 8 7 6 5 4 3 2 1
First Edition

To *Eldene Whiting,*

the teacher who entered my life
at just the right moment

# Contents

# Acknowledgments

*I* WISH TO THANK the many people who have helped in either a direct or indirect way in the writing of this book. Special thanks to Ragnhild Oussoren, who shared her knowledge of Writing-Movement-Therapy, and Joen Gladich, who introduced me to the wonders of form drawing.

To Delina Robair, who allowed me to practice my method at her Educational Tutoring Center, and who continues to support my work.

A very special thank you to my editor, Nathaniel Sherrill, who initially conceived the idea for this book and helped me find a way to present my program to the general public; to my publisher, Jeremy Tarcher, for believing in this project; and to Dianne Woo, for her cooperative effort in the production of this work.

Thank you to my daughter, Breezy, for telling everyone, "Mommy is writing a book!"

To Laurie Fox, for her initial editing and guidance during the first draft.

To Deborah Wiltjer, for her educational expertise.

I also wish to express gratitude to my many graphologist friends who shared both their knowledge and moral support during the writing of this book. Special acknowledgment to Rose Toomey, Linda Larson, Eldene Whiting, Jean Wells, Dr. Patricia Wellingham-Jones, Dr. Ed Peeples, and all the members of the American Handwriting Analysis Foundation and the American Association of Handwriting Analysts. And to the "Eagles," may we all continue to soar.

I give special recognition to my many students who provided me with the proof that this system works.

And a very special thanks to the powers that be—that is, the amazing chain of circumstances that led to the opportunity to write this book.

# How to Use This Book

BETTER HANDWRITING IN 30 DAYS promises you a more legible, attractive, and satisfying personal script, and a deeper understanding of the factors that influence this often overlooked and underappreciated everyday activity. Whether you are a professional, a student, or a teacher or parent of a school-age child, if you have ever been interested in improving your personal script or signature, this is the book for you. It offers an easy-to-follow, step-by-step strategy for understanding what mistakes you make in your handwriting, why you make them, and how you can change them. Even if you already have acceptably legible and readable handwriting, this book explains the graphic impact of your current writing style in ways you may not have ever considered.

The *Better Handwriting* program is based on time-tested, proven handwriting movement exercises and form drawing techniques. The text is presented in two parts. Part One explores the various factors that influence handwriting and addresses the different ways in which handwriting communicates personality to the reader. Part Two introduces and leads you through a form-drawing exercise program that will bring about marked and permanent change in your script and signature by practicing as little as fifteen minutes a day for thirty days.

The number-one reward of better handwriting is improved communication. You will also gain a new appreciation of your handwriting, perhaps even view it as a work of creative self-expression. When receiving handwritten letters or signed memos, you will notice not only the content of the message but the pictoral value of the script as well. Most important, your handwriting will be transformed from an act of boredom or drudgery into one of relaxation and subtle pleasure.

If you are eager to improve your script immediately, you can go directly to Part Two and start the 30-day exercise program. However, I recommend you read Part One not only for the fascinating information it includes on history and writing styles, but because it reveals many of the psychological, physiological, and physical factors that could be hindering your ability to produce a legible script. It is important that you know which, if any, of these factors apply to you before you begin the exercises.

The handwriting improvement strategy of this book is a simple, non-stressful, creative, and relaxing form-drawing program. You will develop more awareness of the elemental shapes that are the basis of all letter forms. You will also begin to see the script style you create with a more artistic eye, and better discern the graphic impression your writing instrument leaves on the paper.

Ideally, you should practice selected exercises every day for at least fifteen minutes. When this is not possible, schedule a longer session to compensate for the days that you miss. As with any kind of practiced discipline, working with minimal distraction will produce the best results. My private consultations with clients usually total only sixty minutes of practice per week.

Once you understand the factors that influence your handwriting and apply the principles described in this book, it will be almost impossible for you *not* to improve your basic handwriting skill. The following stories provide examples of the success you can achieve.

David B., a twenty-eight-year-old college graduate, was starting a new job with an accounting firm and felt his handwriting needed work. Before he undertook the program, David's handwriting had a highly erratic, angular, scrawl-like quality. His sense of movement and connective flow between letters is so deficient that he never achieved anything more than a crude, disconnected printscript. Notice the distortion in his letters *t, l,* and other ascending letter forms. Also, his middle zone letters such as *a, o, e,* and *w* lack any consistency of shape or roundedness, as do many other letters which generally have rounded features. Overall, the irregularity and jagged sharpness of his script make it almost unpleasant to look at.

*David's handwriting before the program*

After our initial meeting, David agreed to participate in the handwriting improvement program in this book, modified to fit a six-week, one-hour-per-week schedule. Because of his maturity and sincere effort, the sessions proceeded smoothly and with noticeable results.

*David's handwriting after the program*

Consider the dramatic improvement in David's handwriting. Most notably, he abandoned his crude printing style and mastered a much more appealing cursive style. Even minute details of his letters changed. Round letters exhibit fullness, ascending and descending letters have strong vertical characteristics, and his spacing and slant are much more consistent. His baseline control on unlined paper is quite acceptable. The result is an exceptionally readable, legible, and personal script that projects an uplifted, friendly quality.

David's results represent the kind of change possible in the handwriting of the average individual. However, the potential for dramatic improvement is also demonstrated by students with special handwriting problems.

One of the most rewarding experiences in my career has been the opportunity to work with foreign students attending English as a Second Language classes. These individuals must learn a new spoken *and* written language and alphabet. Often the left-to-right, top-to-bottom form of written English is completely different from the written form of their native language. The sense of movement and spatial awareness they must develop to write English further complicates the already formidable learning challenges they face in the classroom. Nevertheless, many of these students demonstrate marked progress after only a few sessions in the handwriting improvement program.

Fariba B., a nineteen-year-old Iranian student, shows that improvement is possible for individuals with learning-acquired handwriting problems. Farsi is Fariba's native language, and its written form is rendered in a right-to-left direction—completely opposite of English. Like David, a connected, cursive style was simply beyond Fariba's abilities as she concentrated on the various demands of writing in a new language. Though the legibility of her printscript is fairly acceptable, note the small, static, and constricted quality of her letter forms. The overall effect reflects the plodding, concentrated effort she made to create each letter correctly. Her signature includes some flourishes in her capital letters, but these forms are overwrought and emphasize the lack of style congruence between the signature and the rest of her writing. This sends a confusing visual message to the reader.

*Fariba's handwriting before the program*

Fariba responded immediately to the exercise program and was able to achieve substantial improvement in the pictoral quality of her script. Her subsequent style is a fully developed cursive form with greatly enhanced flow and balance, and increased style congruence of her signature and script. As further testimony to the permanent change that can be achieved, it should be noted that Fariba's second sample was obtained a full year after she finished the six-week hand-writing improvement program. She is presently enrolled in pre-med courses at a community college.

*and I enjoyed taking course with you. Take care of yourself and let's be in touch.*

*Sincerely*
*Fariba Biranvand*

*Fariba's handwriting one year after the program*

As you embark on the 30-day exercise program, I suggest that you read all the chapters first to understand how the sequenced exercises interrelate. Part One will probably give you insight into specific weak-nesses in your handwriting, and you will want to emphasize the exer-cises that apply best to you while de-emphasizing others in areas where your handwriting is strong.

I do not prescribe a specific day-by-day schedule because each writer is different. Depending on how quickly you experience results, you may need to practice one exercise more than others. You should attempt new exercises only when you feel you have done your very best with those already presented and are ready to move on.

Explore this book at your own pace and enjoy. Happy handwriting!

# PART **One**

## *Handwriting Influences and Styles*

# *1*

# *The Handwriting Story and How It Got That Way*

It is scarcely surprising that many of us have outgrown our own handwriting since we learned to form letters and join them up when we were children, and have done very little about our writing since except to make excuses for it. Yet, if we sat down as adults, with almost any one of the handwriting copybooks which can be easily acquired, and gave thought to how we form our letters and to the more natural joins which link them, we could reform our handwriting in an afternoon.

Donald Jackson, *The Story of Writing*

HANDWRITING IS A lost art. The goal of this book is to help you rediscover that art in your personal script and to achieve a more legible, personally expressive style every time you write. In this book you will learn why good, legible handwriting is important and how you can achieve it through a simple, short-term exercise program.

Attempting to improve your handwriting may at first seem like a frivolous thing to do. But it is not. When you consider the many aspects of everyday life in which handwriting is still a necessary form of communication, you see that the consequences of illegible writing can be vast and far-reaching—personally, professionally, financially, and in many other ways. If at this point you still aren't convinced that legible handwriting really matters, a brief look at the price of bad handwriting ought to change your mind.

## COSTS TO YOUR PERSONAL LIFE

Handwriting can affect your personal life in subtle ways. A spat with a loved one can arise because of a sloppily written grocery list. A personal note of love or appreciation may not give a favorable graphic impression if it is hurriedly scrawled or totally illegible. The recipient may think that you don't want to take the time to clearly express your sentiments. What impression do you get when you read each of the following messages? All five say the same thing, but do you feel the same thing expressed in each one?

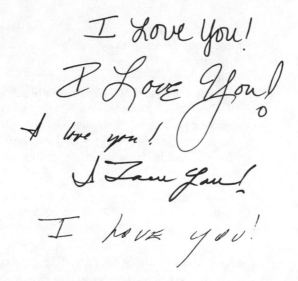

My files are full of love letters and bouquet note cards submitted to me for analysis. In almost every case the recipients sensed that the messages did not correlate with the behavior they were witnessing in their loved one.

Do your personal notes reflect the inner you, or do they send mixed signals to the receiver? Do you receive mixed signals when reading notes from that special someone? In face-to-face meetings, your intuitive feelings can be sparked by many different stimuli—appearance, voice inflection, eye contact, gestures, and body language. You may not have realized it, but you can get, and give, subliminal messages with handwriting as well. The written word provides you with clues to the sender's true feelings. How you choose to respond may mean the difference between a successful relationship and a failed one.

## COSTS TO YOUR PROFESSIONAL LIFE

A significant amount of paperwork may be requested when you apply for a job. Job applications that look sloppy give the impression that the applicant is not well educated or does not have enough interest in the job to write clearly. According to Dr. Sam Toombs, a Houston psychologist, "bad handwriting may be a way of saying something and taking it back at the same time. People scrawl signatures on material for which they don't want to be held responsible." Employee honesty is of great concern to your potential employer. What impression is made when a hiring supervisor can't read what you write, or worse, isn't able to decipher your phone number in order to call you back?

Has a potential employer ever asked you to submit a handwritten cover letter or a writing sample? If so, that company most likely consults with a handwriting analyst when hiring new employees. This procedure is legal. According to the precedent-setting case of *U.S. v. Hazelwood School District,* "handwriting is nondiscriminatory criteria not precluded in hiring if it is related to the job."

## COSTS IN THE WORKPLACE

Have you ever experienced the frustration of trying to decipher a memo or phone message that was totally illegible except for the word *urgent*? Numerous studies indicate that secretaries spend long hours figuring out their bosses' scribbled notes and memos. If you've ever received such a note, or created one for someone else who consequently blew up at you, you can appreciate the importance of communicating clearly and completely in written form at the office.

## COSTS TO THE MEDICAL PROFESSIONS

The handwriting of doctors and dentists is the source of many jokes, but it is serious business. How would you like to take a dose of medicine when the prescription was only guessed at because of the illegibility of the writing? Poor handwriting has been reported to be a leading cause of drug overdose. Pharmacists often become handwriting detectives in order to decipher each quickly scrawled prescription. *Pharmacy Times* magazine even reproduces hopelessly indecipherable orders in an effort to demonstrate the problems poor writing causes.

The *Journal of the American Medical Association* once published the results of research on the handwriting of physicians. The study found that 16 percent of the physicians observed had illegible writing, and 17 percent of them had barely legible handwriting. More than 50 percent of the doctors' writing samples required extra time to interpret because of illegibilities. The researchers concluded that this results in a loss of effective working time for secretaries and nurses.

Furthermore, statistics show that as much as 58 percent of the information on hospital charts and 80 percent of doctors' signatures are illegible. Consider the results of a study summarized in Charles B. Inlander's *Medicine on Trial:*

> Illegible handwriting has an indirect error factor, too: by making progress notes, consultations, and histories and physicals difficult if not impossible to read or understand, physicians set the stage for other subsequent physicians and health care workers to ignore, avoid, or discount these important documents. Also, illegibility on hospital medication orders can necessitate an almost 20 percent "call-back rate." That is, the pharmacy has to send the prescription back to the ordering physician for clarification; thus, time and money and many tempers—if not lives—are lost.

## COSTS IN THE COMMERCIAL SECTOR

Have you ever had to straighten out a billing error on a department-store credit account? How often have you seen your name misspelled on mailing labels?

Bookkeeping errors, garbled records, and botched orders resulting from illegible handwriting all contribute to unnecessary expenses for both the customer and the business owner. Mail-order companies complain of unreadable orders that delay shipment and disrupt cash flow. A restaurant bill often requires a consultation with your server before you are certain it is correct. Annual costs to businesses and consumers amount to a staggering $200 million, not to mention related costs and consumer frustration.

## COSTS TO GOVERNMENT SERVICES

Pity the poor U.S. Postal Service's dead-letter office. The six branches of this department across the country processed almost 90 million pieces of mail in 1987. This task required 337,726 work hours at a cost of nearly $7 million, including salary costs for about 450 "nixie" clerks nationwide, whose sole function is to decipher bad handwriting on letters, packages, and other mailed materials. Yet for all this time and expense, only 6.2 percent of that mail, or 5.58 million pieces, could eventually be delivered. Nearly $875,000 was found in those 90 million pieces of mail, of which only about $50,000 could be forwarded or returned to the sender. The Postal Service has no choice but to pass these losses and unnecessary costs on to the taxpayer in the form of higher rates and slower service. Keep this in mind the next time you or someone you know grumbles about slow postal service.

Hundreds of thousands of tax returns are delayed every year at the Internal Revenue Service because the figures, notes, and signatures on these documents are illegible. These returns are labeled "unpostable" and are set aside until the filers notify the IRS that they have not received their refund. Or even worse, the IRS may pursue the tax-payer for tax evasion if after a certain time period its offices show no record of a return—all because of bad handwriting.

There you have it: billions of dollars of losses in private, public, and government/sectors, and untold losses in our professional and personal lives, all because of sloppy, illegible handwriting. How did handwriting fall into such a dismal state? It's a fascinating story linked to our cultural development; it spans thousands of years, from the time of primitive tribal cultures up to the present.

## THE EVOLUTION OF MODERN HANDWRITING

Our writing heritage is an amalgam of many cultural changes and advances brought on by commerce, conflict, and geography. The earliest record of humankind's nonverbal communication dates as far back as 20,000 B.C. Cave paintings rendered by hunters of the Paleolithic Age and discovered in Lascaux, France, and Altamira, Spain, depict the great beasts of the hunt. The instruments of writing used by these hunter-artists consisted of charcoal and stick brushes; paints were made from powdered minerals mixed with animal fat.

As humankind abandoned the hunt and began to cultivate the land, a more simplified writing form emerged. The Sumerians developed the cuneiform system of wedge-shaped pictograms and ideograms. They also developed the phonogram, a symbol that represents a sound, and the "rebus device," which joins two or more phonograms to make up a word and which is the basis of our written language.

The Egyptians, processing the reeds of the Nile and the papyrus plant for use as writing tools, established the revolutionary use of liquid ink, pen, and paper for their hieroglyphic (picture/symbol) writing.

Our left-to-right writing direction evolved from the Greeks' boustrophedon method, or "as the ox ploughs," which proceeded in alternate right and left directions before the rightward-only mode was adopted. Phoenician merchants introduced a 24-symbol alphabet corresponding to consonant sounds, which provided the basis for our current alphabet.

The Romans developed minuscule and majuscule script, the first alphabet with upper- and lower-case forms. In A.D. 400 the Irish further defined these forms in their magnificently illustrated *Book of Kells.* The more delicate forms of these scripts and the use of parchment and vellum led to the invention of the quill pen, a writing instrument that remained in use until the end of the nineteenth century.

In A.D. 789 the Emperor Charlemagne began a new era of arts and learning. His learned scholar Alcuin of York developed a clear and simple script known as the Carolingian minuscule, which became the root of all succeeding writing styles in our Greco-Roman alphabet.

The Carolingian script evolved further during the Renaissance as handwriting became considered an art form. Then, during the mid-sixteenth century, the ability to write began to be considered beneath a gentleman's dignity. Scribes, secretaries, or cloistered priests were assigned the duty of transcribing, which they carried out in decorative calligraphic styles. The magnificent illuminated texts perserved in the world's great collections were born of this period. The vital role of the scribe began to wane in significance with the invention of the printing press, though many of these skilled craftsmen created new positions for themselves as writing masters, each developing their own copybook style.

In 1733, George Bickham, an Englishman, published *The Universal Penman,* which presented a plain, strong, and neat handwriting style for business and everyday use. English influence was carried to the colonies, and the handwritten documents of our history show evidence of these early serviceable yet decorative styles.

In 1791, soon after U.S. independence, a Bostonian, John Jenkins, published *Art of Writing.* At about the same time a German, Johann Jantssen, developed the steel pen, which was later improved upon by an American from Baltimore, Peregrine Williamson. The machine age provided brisk production of the nib pen. In the 1870s, the world welcomed the invention of the first fountain pen by an American, Lewis Edson Waterman—a name still recognized in the writing industry.

Then the art of handwriting began to decline. New inventions of the industrial age made handwriting seem slow and second-rate. In 1868 the first patent for the typewriter was issued. Thus began the age of technology, which resulted in a gradual decline of interest in the personal, creative aspects of everyday handwriting. In this setting, where human effort was no match for mechanical precision, attractive handwriting soon lost its prestige. Typewriters, dictaphones, manual adding machines, and other mechanical devices signaled the end of classical handwriting art in the same way that photography ended the age of classical painting.

Writing technology was further revolutionized, as well as depersonalized, after World War II with the invention of the ball-point pen by industrialist Middleton Reynolds. Though economical and convenient as a mass-produced product, the ball-point pen eliminated the aesthetic shading once achieved with finer inks and nibs. Since 1945, the writing industry has produced a succession of low-priced writing tools with ball or felt tips. They are cheap and easy to obtain, but their cheap accessibility has further diminished handwriting to a noncreative, nonpersonal, utilitarian mode of communication in an information-hungry society. Typewriters, computers, signature-stamping machines, telephones, and fax machines have elevated the power of mechanically printed information while devaluing the personally expressive element of handwriting.

It is humbling to think that, in a darkened cave, primitive humankind was able to produce breathtaking drawings imbued with potent spiritual meaning that have lasted more than 20,000 years by simply using materials found in nature. We can learn a lot from our early cave-dwelling ancestors. Before each drawing was produced, the artists would first study the cave walls, finding just the right spot. They utilized swellings in the rocks to correspond with the haunches and bellies of the animals depicted. Now the cave wall has become a piece of paper and the charcoal has evolved into a pen, but our innate desire to create meaningful forms through writing seems to be with us still. The renewed practice of calligraphy, the many handwriting-reform movements in education, and the increasing interest in quality writing instruments are all evidence of this.

So, though we can appreciate and utilize advances in technology, we also have the desire to stay in touch with the natural processes that have been with us from the beginning of time. Our reward may be greater than simply more legible handwriting.

## *BETTER HANDWRITING MEANS BETTER COMMUNICATIONS*

Regardless of your specific interest, the number-one reward of newly improved handwriting is better communication with those close to you at work, school, or home.

As you read this book, the inherent personal value of handwriting will make itself clear to you. When your handwriting is legible, your thoughts and ideas will be more easily understood and accepted. The letters you address are less likely to end up in the dead-letter office or shipped off to the wrong zip code. Your checkbook may finally balance when you are able to decipher the names of your creditors and the amounts you spent. Your orders and applications will be processed more quickly. If you are an executive, your letters, notes, and memos may get typed faster and with fewer misinterpreted words.

The accomplished and confident feeling you get when you have made some improvement in your personal appearance, or have received a reward for a job well done, will be the same feeling you experience as you improve your handwriting through the exercise program described in this book.

# CHAPTER 2

# Bad Handwriting: Don't Worry, It's Not Your Fault

> But though I was none the worse for having neglected exercise, I am still paying the penalty of another neglect. I do not know whence I got the notion that good handwriting was not a necessary part of education, but I retained it until I went to England. When later, especially in South Africa, I saw the beautiful handwriting of lawyers and young men born and educated in South Africa, I was ashamed of myself and repented of my neglect. I saw that bad handwriting should be regarded as a sign of an imperfect education.
>
> Mahatma Gandhi

*I*S YOUR WRITING scrawled and illegible? Are you easily fatigued when writing? Are your letter forms contrary to those you were taught in school? No one sets out to produce sloppy handwriting, so what's going on? Factors governing the ability to write clearly and legibly are many and varied. They can be categorized in three basic areas: psychological, physiological, and physical.

Psychological factors include life-style influences, failure in the educational process, and sociocultural differences. Physiological factors range from sensory/motor problems to medically recognized learning disabilities. Physical factors involve general health, seating position, pencil grip, and choice of writing instrument.

The purpose of handwriting is to communicate clearly in written form. If your handwriting isn't totally fulfilling this purpose, most likely the reason can be found in one of these three categories.

## PSYCHOLOGICAL REASONS

At the office the phone rings. The caller has the information you've been waiting for. You grope for a pen while the caller begins his message before you are ready. He's in a hurry, and you're in a hurry. At home, your child needs a note for school and there is but one minute left to get him or her out the door and to the schoolyard on time. Only scraps of paper are available, and every pen in the house seems to be blotchy, scratchy, or dried out. At an important seminar, you are taking notes. The instructor not only speaks rapidly but also has an unfamiliar accent. Your professional future depends on these notes.

It's not hard to figure out that stressful situations like these are not conducive to legible handwriting. Your hectic pace, whether you are at work, home, or school, will be reflected in your handwriting.

### Speed

Writing too quickly is probably the number-one enemy of legible handwriting. Speedy writing tends to end up looking like an unraveled spool of thread or a tangled garden hose. One writer's race to excel reflected the same tempo in his handwriting:

Consider, for example, the daily pace of a doctor: patients scheduled every fifteen minutes, prescriptions and notes scrawled on the way from one room to another, the pressure of decision making while on the go. Doctors have little time to communicate verbally and frequently project this lack of communication in their writing.

*A surgeon's handwriting*

You may not be a doctor, but your life-style may be as rushed as that of a physician on call. However, just slowing down is not necessarily the answer. Finding a rhythm and style that suit your needs is a more comprehensive solution. Part Two of this book will introduce you to exercises that will help you keep pace while getting your message across clearly and legibly.

## Mental and Emotional Problems

Any distortion in your state of mind can, and often will, cause observable distortion in your handwriting. Thus, if you are experiencing severe mental stress, this tension will be evident in your writing. Even when you are only momentarily upset, your handwriting will show it. So don't judge your writing ability too harshly if you are going through some difficult times. Your feelings about the lack of control in your life are directly related to the lack of control in your writing. Instead, set a new daily pace and get in tune with the rhythm of your body. This will help you achieve the same rhythm and balance in your handwriting.

## Your Handwriting Heritage

If your attitude toward your handwriting, or toward handwriting in general, is less than positive—or even downright negative—what is the source of such feelings? Perhaps they are triggered by the mere mention of the word *penmanship*. What sights does this word conjure up? The following might sound familiar to you: *Now, class . . . sit up straight. Put your feet flat on the floor. Put one hand at the top of the page and move the other smoothly across the line.*

Students have been given the same or similar instruction in penmanship for decades. And it always seems to involve the tedious repetition of the same letter form over and over again. In short, it's boring!

To add to the boredom are the classroom environment and the technique with which handwriting is taught. The letters of the alphabet displayed around the classroom stare forebodingly downward at the child, defying duplication. The pressure of the learning environment, with its emphasis on the right form, competition with peers, and the need to meet parental expectations, adds stresses that leave their mark on the young writer. Any eagerness the child may have for learning is further dampened by the child's consequent self-criticism as well as varied levels of comprehension and development.

In *Drawing on the Right Side of the Brain,* Betty Edwards tells us that most adults in our culture who have not studied drawing can draw at only about a ten- to twelve-year-old level. This same phenomenon exists with handwriting as well. The Educational Testing Service reports that among the 2.5 million high-school graduates each year, 25 percent cannot read or write at the eighth-grade level.

I admit that I have met a few unusually compliant souls who have fond memories of the repetitious exercises involved in learning handwriting in school. They seem to have thrived on the tedious adherence to form and rhythm. But this type of compliance is an adaptive behavior that most of us, with our personal quirks and resistances to learning, rarely accept, let alone enjoy.

What is so hard about learning handwriting? Look at this character from the Chinese alphabet. Try to reproduce the form just by looking at the model.

Not easy, is it? Yet teachers hand out worksheets with one letter printed on them and instruct the students to reproduce the form as many times as possible. If you are one of those people who dreaded penmanship class or perhaps never received any formal instruction, your writing and your attitude toward it will certainly be affected. But even if you feel that the system failed you or at least frustrated you beyond the desire to conform, there is still hope for your written communication. The forms and exercises in this book are presented in a nonthreatening way. If you experienced an educational bludgeoning in your early years, I think you will welcome this enjoyable and relaxing way to learn the basic skills of handwriting.

## Handwriting Models of the Past Century

The constant introduction of different writing methods and styles over the past century has also had its effect. What your parents learned in school may be slightly different from the script you learned, and the current generation of schoolchildren may be learning yet another style. One of the earliest widespread methods of handwriting taught in the American school system was Spencerian script. It had originally been developed for commercial use, and it elaborated on the curlicues and swirls of the early nineteenth-century English round hand.

### Spencerian

Your grandparents or great-grandparents probably learned this script, which was introduced into the school system during the nineteenth century. The nib pen and accompanying inkwell were the instruments of writing, and repetition and rote memory were the methods by which students were expected to learn.

The twentieth century saw the introduction of another form of cursive writing, the Palmer method. It was first adopted in the parochial schools, and public schools soon followed suit. The forms used in Palmer are relatively clear but contain many elaborated circles and lead-in strokes that only confuse and frustrate the young learner. You may have been tempted to make some really ornate capital letters or add extra length to the beginning and ending of words if you were given this as your writing model.

## Palmer

A spin-off of the Palmer method was the Zaner-Bloser cursive form, which is similar to both the Palmer method and Spencerian script. If you are a member of the baby-boom generation, some variation of either Palmer or Zaner-Bloser was most likely the school model you learned.

## Zaner-Bloser

At present, many public schools espouse the writing method known as D'Nealian.® It certainly is a vast improvement over the elaborate circle strokes appearing in the Palmer and Zaner-Bloser forms. The D'Nealian® teaching stratagem is to develop a print script that can be easily transformed into cursive writing as early as the second grade.

## D'Nealian®

The lack of a consistent writing method over the years reflects the lack of a standard education policy nationwide, which has caused problems for handwriting students for generations. Due to the highly mobile nature of modern society, your educational history or your child's could include transfers to various schools with noncomplementary or even conflicting approaches to the teaching of handwriting. In addition to having to adjust to these changes, young students frequently miss vital information when their new schedule is out of phase with the schedule of their previous school. The need to relearn a different system with each move would certainly dampen their enthusiasm.

And what if you had been transported to a country where your alphabet did not exist? This plight occurs to the over 600,000 immigrants who come to the United States each year. My eight years' experience as a teacher of English as a second language really brought to light the struggle foreigners face in learning a new language. Learning new letter forms constitutes only part of the challenge. The direction of the writing generates yet another problem. After many years of writing in columns, or in lines from right to left, these students have to master a left-to-right flow.

## *PHYSIOLOGICAL REASONS*

Physiology concerns living organisms and the functions of their parts. The part of the body most associated with the writing process is, of course, the hand. But it does not function as a detached unit. The brain, eyes, and nervous system all contribute to the handwriting process, and when the overall system lacks proper integration, legibility problems develop.

### *Handedness and Dominance*

Which is your normal writing hand? Most likely you are right-handed, since only 10 percent of all Americans are left-handed. The minority status of "lefties" has given them problems through the ages. Early tales associated the left with evil and the devil. Children who displayed a preference for the left hand were greatly encouraged to use their right hand, sometimes more forcefully than necessary. Not only was this approach traumatic, but the forced changes sometimes resulted in reading, speech, and handwriting problems.

You probably have tried writing with your opposite hand just to see how it feels. If you've never done this, try it now. The lack of control you'll experience in your efforts should give you great empathy for those who were forced to change.

If you are right-handed, you will probably be right-footed and right-eyed, with primary language skills in the left brain, and vice-versa if you are left-handed. When there is a mixture of sidedness, you fall into the category known as *cross-dominant*. Children with cross-dominance need to exert extra energy to perform activities such as reading and writing. If you are cross-dominant—and some findings suggest that as many as one in three individuals is—that could explain much of your handwriting problem.

To determine eye dominance, form a triangle with both your hands and focus with eyes open on a specific object in the room. Once you have the item carefully framed, close your left eye. If the object stays in view, you are right-eye dominant. Now try it with your right eye closed. If the object stays in view, you are left-eye dominant. Cross-dominance causes the nondominant eye to pull in the dominant eye's direction during actions like reading and handwriting. Eyestrain and general fatigue are the results, and tension and uneven flow will appear in the cross-dominant individual's handwriting.

Foot dominance can be determined by standing against a wall and simply "putting your best foot forward."

Hand dominance is determined by the hand with which you write, and how you hold your pen. However, only about 40 percent of left-handers show total dominance on the left, with primary language in the right brain. Those who use a hooked left-hand writing style tend to have primary language in the left brain.

Improper handedness can seriously upset the right-brain–left-brain balance when you try to produce handwriting. Sadly, this is frequently the result of change imposed on the writer early in life. This generally occurs when natural left-handers are forced to use their right hand, though there are rare cases in which naturally left-handed individuals simply mimick right-handedness, not following their innate preferences.

## Learning Disabilities

In the methodologies for teaching handwriting, the practice of tracing the letter forms is recommended. This is a wonderful reinforcement for the normal child, but when sensory and perceptual problems exist, the task may be a futile one. Problems with perception, image processing, and directionality, as well as more serious learning disabilities, affect all young writers. If students' specific needs are not met, it is only reasonable to predict that their handwriting will not measure up to standard.

Recent studies by the California Association for Educational Therapists report that 3 to 10 percent of the child population has some type of learning disability, but they believe this figure may even be as high as 20 percent. You may be one of those people. A better term for those who fall into this category is simply *learning different.* Some prevalent problems that specifically affect handwriting are presented here in hopes that you may learn about possible obstacles that have been hindering you, or someone you know, from creating legible handwriting.

*Dyslexia.* Two early and popular symptoms used to define dyslexia are the transposition of letters—especially *d* and *b,* and *p* and *q*—and the practice of mirror writing, or writing backward. But these do not wholly define the dyslexic learner. Many forms of the disorder exist, and varying degrees of success in treating them have been reported. A more technical definition of *dyslexia* is a faulty processing of printed information in the left hemisphere, verbal lobe which causes reading and writing problems. Information goes in just fine; it is the *retrieval* of this information that becomes difficult and frustrating to the learning-handicapped individual.

In their *Dyslexia Determination Test (DDT) Kit,* Drs. John R. Griffin and Howard N. Walton give the following definition of *dyslexia:*

> Minimal brain dysfunction and/or differential brain function manifesting itself as a specific learning disability for language, i.e., reading (decoding), spelling (encoding) and writing (involving graphemes and nemkinesia).

In more common terms, a *grapheme* is a letter of the alphabet, while a *phoneme* is the sound associated with each unit of speech. *Nemkinesia* is the memory of movement required to write the letter shapes from recall. Therefore, the lack of visual memory experienced by dyslexics greatly affects their writing and spelling abilities.

Dyslexia is more complex than most people realize. It affects learning in unique and complicated ways, and its effects on handwriting are clearly evident in the distorted letter forms of those who suffer from it. In my experience in tutoring dyslexics, I have found that the writer's hindered ability to process information makes the writing inconsistent in angle and form.

*My handwriting is not perfect not things, some good, some bad, Kitty*

*Writing of an adult dyslexic*

The dyslexic simply learns in a different way and is not readily adaptable to the traditional methods of written tests and compositions used by our school systems. If you have the feeling that the system was not able to meet your learning needs, your inferior writing and reading ability may be linked to the fact that you are "learning different."

*Dysgraphia.* This problem is specifically related to handwriting. Dysgraphia is the inability to execute the motor movements required to write or copy written letters or forms, or the inability to transfer the input of visual information to the output of fine motor movement. It can also be a combination of both of these conditions. In short, your hand won't cooperate with your brain. You see the letter form clearly, but you can't transfer the image to paper via your writing hand.

If you or your teachers were never quite satisfied with your penmanship, you may have some level of dysgraphia. I have seen dysgraphic script that ranges from immature forms and periodic patching to totally illegible scrawling.

Some examples of suspected dysgraphic writers:

*Writing of a seven-year-old girl*

*Writing of an eleven-year-old boy*

*Writing of a twelve-year-old boy*

*Writing of an adult*

21

When you consider the importance of handwriting as a form of self-expression, you can then understand how the self-esteem and personal self-worth of dysgraphics have been affected by their inability to write clearly and legibly.

Other physiological conditions as defined by Samuel T. Orton in his book *Reading, Writing and Speech Problems in Children* are:

*Finger agnosia.* The body is a system of complex parts and connections. When just one of these connections short-circuits, it can result in some very dynamic physiological road blocks. Think about how a "normal" writer first begins to write. The image is taken into the brain via the eye, processed through the brain, and sent down through the arm to the nerve endings in the hand. All goes well until the image comes to the very tip of the fingers. It is here that the writer grasps the writing instrument and begins to express the pictures of his mind on paper. If that writing instrument is not held properly, the incorrect pen pressure results in varying levels of control and depth of the writing.

Finger agnosia is a condition that causes a loss of the power to recognize the import of sensation. You just can't feel the pen in your hand. This causes inconsistent shading and unnatural twisting of the writing instrument. If you are one of those people who can bite their nails down to the quick and not feel a thing, you may be lacking the tactile skill necessary to efficiently move the pen across the paper.

I hate him
he says I'm Dann

*Writing displaying symptoms of finger agnosia*

A good test for finger agnosia is to mentally number your fingers from one to five, beginning with the thumb. Close your eyes and have someone gently touch the tips of your fingers and see if you can tell which number corresponds to the finger being touched. Your success in handwriting may depend on your success in passing this simple tactile exam.

*Aphasia.* Have you ever suffered a head trauma? If so, you may have recovered nicely, but you may have acquired an aphasic condition in the process. Acquired aphasia is a loss in the power of expression by speech, writing, or signs, or of comprehending spoken or written language due to injury or disease of the brain centers. Your motor skills are carefully monitored by specialists after a major brain injury or surgery. But if you were not sufficiently rehabilitated, you may well be a victim of acquired aphasia.

Developmental aphasia is a condition present from birth. According to Orton, it is "a failure in the development of speech or speech understanding which is not the result of deafness or of defect in the peripheral speech mechanism." If you cannot clearly understand what is being said or shown to you, you certainly cannot reproduce it with any high degree of accuracy. If your condition was congenital, then somewhere along the line you most likely were identified as learning disabled and unceremoniously plunked into a special class.

*Developmental apraxia.* Have you ever felt that you were all thumbs? Have people made reference to your being doubly left-handed? In either case, you may have some type of dexterity problem. The disorder known as developmental (or congenital) apraxia may explain your lack of coordination. Defined by Orton as "a failure in development of normal skills, abnormal clumsiness," apraxia is grouped with the disorders affecting handwriting because it sometimes incorporates dysgraphia. The apraxia sufferers' clumsiness is usually reflected in their writing since they are unable to establish dominance on either side of their body.

Sadly, the suggested method of dealing with apraxia is to wait for the sufferer to grow out of it. One of my students, a young man of fourteen, had such ego-defeating experiences in the public-school system that his apraxia was becoming life-threatening. For an entire year, he had to be hospitalized for severe depression. Today, though he has overcome debilitating depression, he still lacks self-esteem and continues to resist tutoring. Intuitively, he knows that he cannot reproduce what I ask of him and so engages in distracting activities to avoid having to perform. The teases and taunts of his fellow schoolmates have made him defensive and uncooperative. However, with a definite diagnosis, he can now petition the school to allow him to take oral tests.

*Rle I had H ngrn pest and I pased*

*Writing of a fourteen-year-old apraxic-dysgraphic*

If you were constantly taunted by parents, teachers, and classmates because you unknowingly suffered from apraxia, by now you have most likely grown out of it. So choose a dominant side to write with, and use this book to reteach yourself the writing skills that eluded you in your earlier years.

*Developmental Gerstmann syndrome.* This condition has been recognized only in the past fifty years and affects nearly every skill that is necessary for successful learning within a compulsory teaching system. Developmental Gerstmann syndrome, as defined by Dr. John H. Richards of Kaiser Permanente Center for School Problems, is "the problem of appreciating your position in space so as to order or sequence objects or ideas around you to make relative sense out of environmental demands." If you can't tell right from left and have problems organizing numbers and letters, you might be a victim of Gerstmann syndrome.

Gerstmann syndrome encompasses other dysfunctions, including dyscalculia (problems with numerical manipulation) and dysgraphia. It is, however, somewhat rare and seems to surface around the fourth grade, when greater demand is placed on the child. At this grade level, the student encodes his learning through written work, logic, and greater efficiency of expression. The student with developmental Gerstmann syndrome can, on some days, produce acceptable work and on other days has what appears to be a total breakdown of information processing and reproducing. This condition often prompts the teacher to think that the student, though capable, just isn't trying.

As rare as this condition is, I have encountered its symptoms in an eleven-year-old male student referred to me for special handwriting tutoring by a learning-disability specialist. At this point, no specific disability had been diagnosed in the boy, who was attending a special-education class for math and had completed an adaptive physical-education class.

Our sessions began with the normal handwriting-movement exercises that I use with most students. As the student began to make connected loops on the blackboard, I noticed that the chalk had worn down, but he continued to drag his fingers across the slate. I quickly administered the finger-agnosia test and found that he had no feeling in the tips of his fingers. He also could not determine where a normal page of writing should begin and end. I asked the mother to take her son for a physical checkup that would focus on these observed problems. His physician of ten years diagnosed his learning problem as that of Gerstmann syndrome.

*Writing of a child with Gerstmann syndrome*

Once the presence of Gerstmann syndrome has been established in students, they can petition the school system to be allowed to take their tests orally. Most sufferers of this syndrome do grow out of it to some extent, but unfortunately they are being taught to write when the condition is at its worst.

## PHYSICAL REASONS

The most common physical problem shared by poor writers is in the actual relationship between the person, the pen, and the page. Selection of the best writing instrument, pen grip, and writing posture will be discussed in more detail in chapters 5 and 11. However, you should know now that using a faulty writing instrument and poor pen grip and posture will have a big effect on the mechanical act of handwriting and on the appearance of the finished product, regardless of your handwriting skills.

How are you feeling physically? There is no point in worrying about the beauty of your script if you are not feeling well. Illness results in low physical energy, which translates into slowness and lack of vitality in your script. The physical weakness associated with illness affects writing pressure. Your writing will appear as weak and lethargic as you feel.

*I have a touch of the flu today and don't feel much like writing.*

*Writing of someone suffering from the flu*

Chronic conditions, however, make legibility an ongoing problem. Writers with chronic conditions such as arthritis and other muscle and joint ailments suffer from interference with the flow of their normal handwriting all the time.

*Margaret, Kathy and I will travel to Europe. What fun we will have!*

*Writing of someone with arthritis*

Trigger thumb is another condition resulting from physical problems in the hand. A trait that places us high on the evolutionary scale is our opposable thumb, which improves our ability to grasp objects. Trigger thumb exists when a bump in the thumb's flexor tendon causes a triggering or popping of the thumb, which reduces a person's ability to hold a pen for long periods of time. Writing fatigue sets in quickly and causes obvious problems in handwriting.

*I have to tell you I dread writing because of my "trigger thumb." The tension*

*Writing of someone with trigger thumb*

## SOLUTIONS

Modern psychological theory contends that many problems can be resolved when people learn to modify their responses. In this perspective, a split second of forethought can make the difference between a nonproductive overreaction and a more mature perspective on a situation. This book offers exercises related to relaxation, coordination, breathing, and balance that will help anyone dispel the stress-related deterrents to good handwriting. Who knows? You may even develop an intuitive sense of your inner feelings through working on your handwriting.

The problems of cross-dominance and related physiological blockages can be treated by a therapeutic process known as sensory-motor integration (SMI). As its name suggests, this is an attempt to balance the input to the senses with the motor output of the impressions they receive. Information on SMI can be obtained from Sensory Integration International (1402 Cravens Ave., Torrance, CA 90501). One of the best sources of information on disabilities related to dyslexia is the Orton Dyslexia Society, which has branches throughout the United States. (Its international headquarters are at 724 York Rd., Baltimore, MD 21204; phone 800/ABCD123.)

If you suspect your child has a learning problem, Public Law 94-142 gives you the legal right to request testing for your child through the public school system. The school must then take the responsibility of studying and interpreting these results in order to design an Individual Educational Program (IEP) to meet your child's specific needs. For detailed information about your legal rights, contact Educators Publishing Service at 75 Moulton St., Cambridge, MA 02138.

For physical problems, it is best simply to be cognizant of your limitations. If you are sick, injured, or otherwise disabled, let the reader know this, apologizing only once for your less-than-perfect handwriting. The elements you do have control over such as pen, paper, and writing position should be utilized to the best of your ability and opportunity. (More on this in chapters 5 and 11.)

CHAPTER *3*

## *Your Handwriting as a Form of Self-Expression*

> Every thing in man is progressive; every thing congenial; form, stature, complexion, hair, veins, nerves, bones, voice, walk, manner, style, passion, love, hatred. One and the same spirit is manifest in all.
>
> Johann Kasper Lavater, physiognomist

*H*AVE YOU EVER wondered why your handwriting remains uniquely yours, despite momentary changes? We'll consider this question now, and through it develop a new way of looking at handwriting that will help you improve your script.

Even if your handwriting is rarely if ever affected by the many external factors described in the previous chapter, it will always be uniquely yours because of an internal factor not yet discussed. Present in each of us is a highly complex, magical essence formed by experience, conditioning, genetic inheritance, and other basic factors. We call it personality. This chapter is based on the premise that personality influences handwriting.

Some people feel that handwriting reflects the writer's actual personality in extreme detail, that through a handwriting sample one can obtain a complete psychological and physical profile of the writer. Others contend that there is no way to test this theory scientifically. Still others will not admit the possibility at all.

What I am convinced of, after years of experience working with hundreds of clients, is that handwriting *itself* has personality. Handwriting—a full page, a line, a signature, a word, even one letter— makes a personality connection *in the mind of the reader.* In this context, the question is not "Am I expressing my personality in my handwriting?" but "What can I do to assure that I will be communicating my intended meaning fully and richly to my reader?"

Does the idea of the personality connection in handwriting seem odd or curious to you? In the following matching test, select the handwriting that you feel best expresses the personality traits listed with each set of examples.

1. A *fully this sample is sufficient*

   B *I wish I could read you*

   _____ leader     _____ follower

2. A togе+ in on your special but I have

   B *Once a year isn't bad for us*

   _____ people-oriented     _____ things-oriented

3. A the same info that's on the listing + tell them when + where it will be.

   B *Escribiпе Eu*

   _____ artistic     _____ analytical

Answers: 1. A, B  2. B, A  3. B, A

How did you fare? Probably pretty well. Frequently my lecture audiences will correctly match the samples and traits with 100 percent accuracy. More important, the demonstration highlights one of the most essential qualities about handwriting: it expresses personality. Our goal in this book is to enhance the readability of your script, and your inner satisfaction in creating it. To do that we will focus our attention not on your personality, but on the personality expressed in your handwriting. We will develop specific corrective actions to improve legibility, which will in turn allow you to produce a self-expressive, communicative, personal script.

## SELF-EXPRESSION AND THE PERSONALITY CONNECTION

We present ourselves to the world in many different ways. How we dress and wear our hair, the way we walk and talk, our gestures, facial expressions, and body language, the car we drive, and even our handwriting, all give nonverbal clues about who we are and how we would like to be perceived.

Entire industries have grown up around our desire to express ourselves more effectively. Certainly the multi-billion-dollar fashion industry thrives on our desire to express a dynamic personal image and style. Books, cassette courses, and private video consultations advise individuals on everything from how to behave like a successful manager in business to how to attract the perfect mate. We can even have our appearance analyzed in order to know our most effective "colors" and "seasons."

This chapter opened with a quote from the famous physiognomist Johann Kasper Lavater, a man who devoted himself to studying the relationship between personal character, mental qualities, and body features. Though physiognomy is not considered a scientifically valid method for studying personality, you need only visit a shopping mall on a busy Saturday afternoon to discover that we all are physiognomists to a certain degree. As chronic "body watchers," we automatically interpret the character of people by observing their appearance, how they carry themselves, and many other kinds of self-expressive movements, including handwriting. Given the inevitability of body watching, two very important questions can be asked that relate to the issue of handwriting and personality. First, are the many self-expressive acts of everyday life imbued with qualities related to personality? And second, how reliable or accurate is the interpretation of personality through body watching?

Answers to these and other related questions were found by two highly respected research psychologists, Gordon W. Allport and

Philip E. Vernon, in a landmark study on expressive movement in humans. Allport and Vernon addressed a long-standing scientific debate regarding the relationship between personality and body movement. One school of thought supports what can be called the "personalistic" view, according to which the psychological aspects of personality influence motor skills. The opposing, "mechanistic," view limits influencing factors in motor skills to physical conditions in the body.

In their study, Allport and Vernon observed, recorded, analyzed, and quantified a wide variety of self-expressive movements among the members of their study group, including how the individuals expressed themselves when talking, laughing, weeping, and gesturing, and through handwriting. Also noted and measured were other related personality traits, such as the subjects' likes and dislikes, furnishings, dress, and even nicknames. The findings of the study were published in a book entitled *Studies in Expressive Movement,* which includes a summary that states:

> Fundamentally our results lend support to the personalistic contentions that there is some degree of unity in personality, that this unity is reflected in expression, and that, for this reason, acts and habits of expression show a certain consistency among themselves.

In other words, a particular trait in your personality makeup will appear to have a consistent influence on all your self-expressive actions, including handwriting.

Allport and Vernon's published findings included the results of their study directed specifically at the relationship of handwriting to personality. This study involved a handwriting matching test similar to the one you took at the beginning of this chapter, but executed under much more precise scientific control.

For Allport and Vernon's test, three groups of "judges" were selected. The first group consisted of 143 male undergraduates; the second, 25 members of a college faculty; and the third, 17 professional graphologists, or handwriting analysts. The judges' task was to match ten personality descriptions with ten samples of handwriting. The subjects in this experiment were selected mostly from the faculty and graduate-student population at the university where the study took place, but included other individuals from diverse social and educational backgrounds.

The findings showed that all three groups of judges were able to match the writings with the personality descriptions at a rate higher than chance. More important, it was observed that all three groups achieved their highest matching success rates when comparing handwriting samples from the most diverse personality types among the subjects. This was particularly true in regard to the two most diverse subjects, a noted theological scholar and a barber. Allport and Vernon's closing statement concluded:

> The more unlike two personalities, the less frequently are their handwritings mistaken, and the more similar they are in some essential characteristic, the more often are their handwritings confused.

How does this information help us reach our goal of improved handwriting? Improving your handwriting requires that you first develop a more skillful way of looking at it. Allport and Vernon's study revealed such a way: the judges most successful overall in the matching experiment were the graphologists. Regardless of whether you believe that graphology as a study is accurate, graphologists use a highly articulated, systematic approach to *looking* at handwriting. Looking at your handwriting carefully is the first step in improving its legibility. Also, if you accept that handwriting projects personality of some kind to a reader, you will benefit from simply refocusing the graphological approach. By using graphological principles, you can assess from a reader's standpoint the personality of your handwriting *itself.*

## DISCOVERING THE PERSONALITY IN YOUR HANDWRITING

We start by assuming that your handwriting projects personality of some kind to the reader. That essence of personality, depending on the situation, may or may not accurately reflect your true personality. In either case, we intend to improve the legibility of your script.

According to the new view of handwriting described here, this highly personal expressive act is much more than simply ink on paper. To begin with, a blank sheet of paper signifies more than a thin sheet of processed, dried wood pulp lying on your desk or writing table. In truth, a piece of paper comes with a complex spectrum of psychological associations and relative values associated with space, time, and directionality. It represents the environment of the writer. These associations relate to the way in which we visually enter any page of written or printed material.

You may now consider your handwriting as merely generic letter groups spread in two dimensions across the width and height of a blank piece of paper. It is actually a kind of "crystallized gesture" inscribed in three dimensions. Not only does it lie across the surface width and height of the paper, but it extends *into* the paper when extra pen pressure is applied. You can see proof of this by simply looking at the reverse side of any handwriting sample. Points of greater pressure in the writing will appear as tiny peaks pressing through the paper, sometimes even penetrating it. The handwriting act also includes movements of the pen tip *above* the paper, referred to as airstrokes. This unrecorded portion of the stroke bridges the gap between the point from which the pen is raised from the paper to the point at which it returns.

We might even say that there is a fourth dimension to handwriting: time. Like any other action in time, handwriting includes a beginning and an end, and, by implication, associations related to the concept of past, present, and future. Handwriting creates a frozen graphic image of the writer's self-expression at one particular moment.

The three guiding principles that project the personality in any handwriting sample are arrangement, form, and movement. As you read this chapter, consider how the terms may apply to your handwriting. This will help you set some personal-improvement goals to work toward in the second half of the book.

## *Arrangement*

Arrangement refers to how the writing is placed on the page and includes the concepts of zones, margins, slant, baseline, and spacing. It concerns the standard practices of your "paper presence." A blank page symbolizes a writer's space, environment, and territory. Just as a visitor chooses how to occupy physical space when entering a room, a writer chooses to occupy the blank page with handwriting. Would you enter a client's office doing cartwheels and then lean against the wall at a forty-five–degree angle? Obviously not. If writing to this person, would you want to create the same effect in your handwriting? Again, obviously not. And yet you would be surprised how often handwriting makes just such impressions.

From the graphic-design perspective, the elements of arrangement are very similar to the design elements considered by production designers and other graphic artists every time they create advertisements or other graphic expressions in any kind of print media. When you think about a page of your writing from this perspective, you can easily see why a well-balanced arrangement on the page makes a favorable presentation of your message and of you.

*The three handwriting zones.* When learning to write as children, we simply accept that different letters have different shapes. As adults we tend to look at each letter as a whole symbol, with little thought given to the space it occupies. Understanding the zonal aspects of handwriting will help you see the spatial significance of the letters you create.

Three handwriting zones exist in every line of script that you write. They are, simply, the Middle, Upper, and Lower zones. The Middle Zone is referenced first because all the letters of the alphabet begin or pass through it as they are created.

Middle Zone letters include *a, c, e, i, m, n, o, r, s, u, v, w,* and *x.*
Letters considered Upper Zone are *b, d, h, k, l,* and *t.*
The Lower Zone consists of the letters *g, j, p, q, y,* and *z.*
The letter *f* is the only trizonal letter, meaning that it occupies all three writing zones.

In their study of expressive movement, Allport and Vernon incorporated both physical and psychological characteristics when defining the personalities of the members of their study group. In the same way, the three letter zones correspond to specific physical and psychological aspects of the "body" and personality of your handwriting, as is demonstrated by this chart:

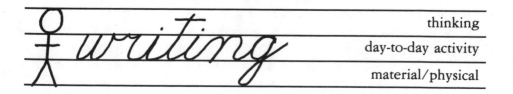

| | |
|---|---|
| | thinking |
| | day-to-day activity |
| | material/physical |

The Middle Zone corresponds to the torso of the script "body." It is the most emphasized area of writing, since all letters must pass through it. This area of a script projects to the reader the ego dynamics of the writer and the everyday need for activity, achievement, and attention. The size of the Middle Zone firmly demonstrates the modesty or flamboyance of the writer's physical presence.

The Upper Zone can be considered the "head" of the script and expresses qualities of intellect to the reader. Extreme extensions of script in the Upper Zone can imbue it with an air of great intellectual and philosophical knowledge. Other personality traits it can project are open-mindedness, illusions, and delusion. Qualities of imagination and spiritual ideals or character are also expressed in the Upper Zone.

The Lower Zone corresponds to the "legs" of the script and evokes a sense of material or physical interest. It can project qualities of creativity or suggest fantasies and instinctual drives. It expresses subconscious motivational factors such as the love of money, sexual drive, and the desire for material gain.

The following lists explain the various psychological associations these three zones can impart to the reader.

| *Upper Zone* | *Middle Zone* | *Lower Zone* |
|---|---|---|
| Spirit | Mind | Body |
| Intangible | Practical | Tangible |
| Intellect | Ego | Id |
| Imagination | Impetus | Action |
| Ideals | Emotion | Drive |
| Theory | Habit | Instinct |
| Cultural | Social | Material |
| Philosophy | Conscious awareness | Subconscious |

This simple overview of zonal significance gives you the basis for your new personalistic view of handwriting. There are no hard and fast rules in regard to script personality, only general concepts for you to consider.

*Margins.* Margins are defined by the boundaries writers create as they first enter and subsequently conclude their occupation of the writing environment. The blank space left around a page of handwriting constitutes each writer's preferred distance for both the right and left and the top and bottom margins.

While not central to the quality of legibility in your script, margins contribute much to the overall impression made on your reader. Balanced, intentionally composed margins promote clear communication and project qualities of organization, skill, clarity, mastery, and professionalism. Erratic or poorly placed margin space communicates any number of qualities such as disorganization, inconsistency, hesitance, compulsiveness, and unpredictability. Margins also suggest relationship between the writing and the element of time. Does your script give the impression of being well balanced and centered in the "now" of the middle of the page? Does it seem to cling to the left, as if it were afraid to venture into the future? Or is it racing off the far side of the page in a rush, as if it were behind schedule or caught up in some ungrounded future fantasy?

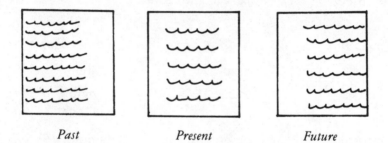

| Past | Present | Future |

*Slant.* Slant refers to the angle of specific letters and also to the overall impression of slant conveyed by a complete sample of your script. Not only does it suggest personality characteristics, but it has much to do with legibility.

Whatever angle of slant you choose, consistency in that angle will be one of your writing-improvement goals. By maintaining consistent slant, your script appears to flow across the page with grace, stability, and control. Fluctuations in slant angle suggest uncertainty, vacillation, and lack of control. The following list correlates slant with associations your reader is likely to make.

| *Left Slant* | *Vertical Slant* | *Right Slant* |
|---|---|---|
| Past | Present | Future |
| Origins | Day-to-day activity | Goals |
| Passive | Active | Aggressive |
| Self | Things | Others |
| Security | Independence | Authority |
| Introvert | Control | Extrovert |

*This is left slant.*

Left slant—past

*This is vertical slant*

Vertical slant—present

*This is right slant.*

Right slant—future

*Baseline.* Baseline refers to the imaginary line upon which writers place their script when writing across the page. Radical baseline fluctuations have much the same effect on the character of your script as erratic margins and slant, except that they project more of an emotional state. For instance, an upward-slanting baseline is often interpreted as a sign of optimism, while a downward-slanting baseline may project pessimism or negativity.

The more erratic the baseline, the more emotional the script will appear, and since there is no way to determine exactly which emotion is in play (although other elements in the script may make this clear), the erratic baseline simply makes your reader uncomfortable.

*A straight baseline is calm.*

Straight baseline—calm emotional state

*An upward baseline is optimistic.*

Upward baseline—optimism

*A downward baseline is pessimistic.*

Downward baseline—pessimism

*An erratic baseline is upsetting.*

Erratic baseline—upset emotional state

*Spacing.* Spacing refers to the distance between letters in a word, between words in a line, and between lines on a page. Cramped or tight letter forms make handwriting unattractive and difficult to read. They project thriftiness or tension. Widely spaced letters, on the other hand, can suggest extravagance or ease.

*wide letter*

Wide letter spacing—extravagant/relaxed

*narrow letter space*

Narrow letter spacing—thrifty/tense

Spacing between words communicates a writer's territorial claim for himself in relationship to other people. Widely spaced words can give the reader an impression of social distancing and aloofness, while narrowly spaced words can imply overfamiliarity and a lack of social timing. Words surrounded by relatively more space than others will appear highlighted in the reader's eye, and though this effect may register only subliminally, any number of messages may be communicated, depending on the word itself.

*wide word spacing.*

Wide word spacing—need for social distance

*medium word spacing.*

Medium word spacing—socially responsive

*narrow word spacing.*

Narrow word spacing—overfamiliar in social situations

Space between lines is a compositional skill similar to margin placement. The even, proportionally balanced spacing between lines that promotes the legibility we seek projects organization, directedness, clarity of thought, and other worthy traits.

*handwriting that is clearly spaced looks more legible.*

Clear spacing between lines

When the space between each line of writing is inconsistent, it has the same impact as poor slant and lack of baseline control, and is only compounded when the letter forms in these lines entangle. Entangled lines project the feeling of ideas in collision—the result of confusion, indecision, or both.

*handwriting that happens to to intertangle can look messy.*

*Entangled lines*

## Form

The second guiding principle in your new view of handwriting is form. In this context, form refers to the actual shape of the letters and the connective strokes that join them.

*Form level.* Have you ever received a letter and been impressed with the neatness and style of the writing, or received one that was so erratic and messy that you had difficulty deciphering it? What you respond to in the letters you receive and what the judges in the Allport–Vernon study responded to is what is known as the form level of handwriting.

Form level is the picture value of handwriting—whether the script gives an overall impression of neatness or sloppiness, whether it has originality or appears ordinary. This is the aspect of handwriting that expresses the most aesthetic and cultural qualities in the script. High form level in handwriting is created by balanced zonal forms, rhythm in the baseline, and consistent slant and strokes, as well as the individual's personal style of writing. A low form level is created when these factors are lacking.

*Well, here is an example of my hand-writing. Is it full form? Does the fact*

*High form level writing*

*This is the time for all good men to come to the aid of their*

*Low form level writing*

In considering style and form level, we will define four primary handwriting styles and illustrate the impression their high and low form levels impart to the reader. This will establish the basis of the exercises in Part Two of this book.

*Connectives and the four primary handwriting styles.* *Connectives* is a general term referring to the strokes that connect letters into words. Just as skill is required to form letters clearly, skill level affects your connective strokes, and this in turn influences the personality expressed in your handwriting. You may not have given much thought to these seemingly insignificant strokes in your handwriting, yet connectives are very important to its legibility and flow.

Connectives are also essential in shaping each letter and can be found not only between letters, but within them and in the beginning and ending strokes of each word. All the various kinds of connective relationships, and all the various ways that writers express connective forms, can be grouped into four basic categories, which correlate to the four primary handwriting styles we will discuss in this book.

### The Primary Connective Forms

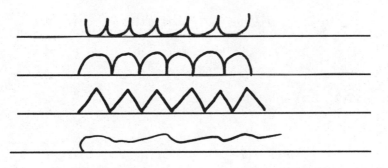

The Garland Style incorporates connective forms that are cuplike and rounded. To form a visual impression of this style, think of the garlands draped around a Christmas tree. Generally, the Garland Style expresses empathy or naivety, depending on its form level.

### *High Form Level—Garland Style (Empathy)*

*Do you need a secretary? I need a job! I'm very organized and I'd*

### *Low Form Level—Garland Style (Naivety)*

*fun! Did you write these crazy sentences quickly?*

The Arcade Style incorporates connective forms that are curved up and over (really an inverted Garland form). To form a visual impression of this style, think of the archways in a Spanish-style church. Generally, the Arcade Style expresses creativity or defensiveness, depending on its form level.

### *High Form Level—Arcade Style (Creativity)*

*This is my normal handwriting. May this be the merriest of*

### *Low Form Level—Arcade Style (Defensiveness)*

*What fun we will*

The Angle Style emphasizes sharp, pointed strokes along the baseline and in the tops of some letters such as the *m*s and *n*s. To form a visual impression of this style, think of a line of dramatic, sharply

outlined peaks of a mountain range. The Angle Style expresses ana-.
lytic power or criticism, depending on its form level.

*High Form Level—Angle Style (Analytic Power)*

*My handwriting is not perfect nor poor,*
*this, some good, some bad.*

*Low Form Level—Angle Style (Criticism)*

*Europe. What fun we will have.*

The Thread Style emphasizes compressed vertical and stretched
horizontal connectives. To form a visual impression of this style, think
of a coiled garden hose that has been stretched out to full length across
the ground, or an unwinding ball of string. The Thread Style expresses diplomacy or evasiveness, depending on its form level.

*High Form Level—Thread Style (Diplomacy)*

*to have a lot of fun. I love*

*Low Form Level—Thread Style (Evasiveness)*

*to Europe what fun we*
*have. I love*

## Movement

Movement refers to the energy projected in the writing, a quality
determined primarily by the factors of speed and pressure in the
writing style.

*Speed.* Speed refers to both the rate at which a script is produced and the pace of the script, as it is projected to the reader. It is the single most frequent cause of illegible handwriting. But it is also a relative concept. A writing rate that is too slow for you might be too fast for someone else. There is no right or wrong speed, only the rate and appearance that feel right to you. Generally, we all write too quickly and would benefit by giving our handwriting just a split second more time and care.

Slowness in the rate or pace of handwriting does not necessarily express lack of intelligence. Rather, it tends to give a feeling of careful, cumulative thinking. Slow, calculated writing that looks attractive may also be the work of a cunning, deceitful writer.

If you suspect you haven't found your own rate and pace of handwriting, the exercises in this book will help you find them, particularly if the exercises are performed to music. This will be discussed further in Part Two.

### High Form Level—Fast Speed

*I've never had my handwriting analyzed*

### Low Form Level—Fast Speed

*So he is going to stop in to see me, while he*

### High Form Level—Slow Speed

*Margaret, Katy & I will travel to Europe.*

## *Low Form Level—Slow Speed*

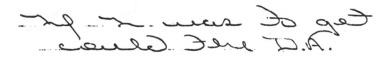

*Pressure.* Pressure refers to the amount of downward force applied to the writing instrument during the handwriting process. If you haven't studied the reverse side of a handwriting sample, do so now. A sample made with standard stock paper and a sharp ball-point pen will offer the best evidence of writing pressure. Forgery experts always make a point of studying the pressure points and ridges visible in handwriting samples. Pen pressure presents itself in a pattern of movement so reliable that it can literally separate the innocent from the guilty.

Pressure in handwriting projects emotional intensity and conveys qualities of health and vitality. Light writing pressure combined with weak letter forms will convey lethargy, thus diminishing the impact of the information. Excessively heavy pressure, on the other hand, will disrupt the writing flow.

Frequently pressure effects are not the result of the writer's efforts, or lack thereof, but are more a function of the writing instrument used. Broad felt-tip pens, especially if they are softened with wear, will mark a wide, heavy line regardless of the pressure applied. This is a clear example of the little-regarded fact that pens have a personality all their own that may serve or disserve your own writing style.

## INTERPRETING YOUR RESULTS

Do you recognize aspects of your own handwriting style in the examples in this chapter? If you do, you're already ahead of the game. But if you don't yet see your personal style, perhaps it's because of negative, judgmental experiences in your handwriting heritage.

To reiterate the philosophy of this book, understand that there is no "right" or "wrong" writing style for you or anyone else. You are probably already using a style, or combination of styles, that is most comfortable for you. Any connective style can be a positive, legible, and expressive one. In the next chapter, I would like to offer you entertaining and illuminating proof of the positive value of all writing styles, and the personalities they project. Then we can move on to exercises designed to give you the handwriting style you desire.

# CHAPTER 4

# *What's Your Writing Style?*

It is most true—our style betrays us.
Robert Burton, English clergyman and author

You NOW KNOW why your handwriting is an important, personally expressive act, and you know enough about how to observe its strong and weak graphic elements to determine your own writing style. This is important, since it will help you determine which exercises in Part Two will be most relevant to your particular needs.

In this chapter you will compare your writing with some distinct styles exhibiting common weaknesses in order to determine which areas of your style deserve special attention. How should you approach critiquing your handwriting? Lightly, and in good cheer. As a handwriting consultant, I encounter many people who express strong dislike for their writing even though it is reasonably legible and of a high form level. Such self-critical attitudes have no place in this book, so leave them out.

Go easy on yourself, and remember that this process is supposed to be fun *and* beneficial. Dislike of your handwriting may signal deeper psychological conflicts involving a general lack of self-confidence or self-esteem. Unfortunately, the anxieties generated by such stressful, self-castigating attitudes only cause your handwriting to deviate even more from how you would like it to be. But don't worry. Part Two takes into consideration these kinds of stressful attitudes. The exercises found there will help you not only improve your handwriting but also incorporate relaxation techniques that can assist you in overcoming the effects of self-critical feelings.

To get started, find a representative sample of your writing. If nothing is available to you, or if you would like to start with a fresh sample (that's the enthusiastic spirit!), on an unlined sheet of paper, using a pen with which you are comfortable, write—don't print—the following sentence:

I can communicate through my handwriting.

If you would like to write more than this, please feel free to do so. More sentences give you extra material to work with, and they will demonstrate how fatigue affects your writing. When you are finished, sign your name and date the sample.

Take a good look at your sample. Do you like it or dislike it? What don't you like about it? How did you feel when you wrote it? How do you feel about yourself while looking at it? Are you more comfortable with printing? Did you experience any physical discomfort when writing? What thoughts come to mind as you consider your handwriting in light of what you've learned in this book so far? You may even want to write these thoughts down as part of your writing sample. This sheet will remain valuable to you throughout Part Two, and represents the first sample that can be compared to the progressive improvement you will experience in your handwriting.

The writing styles to be shown and described in this chapter are based on the four connective forms discussed in chapter 3: the Garland, Arcade, Angle, and Thread Styles. As you consider these different styles, remember that your writing could contain elements of several styles. But in any case you should be able to isolate the forms that apply to your writing.

Please don't feel intimidated about your handwriting. There is no need to be. Perfect-looking handwriting is no insurance of fame, fortune, health, or anything else—except good communication. Throughout history people have achieved greatness despite weak, even deplorable handwriting skills. On the other hand, as you discover your writing style, you may be pleasantly surprised to find that some highly accomplished people also share your style of writing.

## *GARLANDS: THE EMPATHETIC WRITER*

Garland writing contains many cuplike formations that tend to overemphasize the roundedness of letters. If your handwriting sample reveals softly rounded letter forms that lack originality, your style may put you into one of two general categories: the Bubble writer and the Passive writer. Here are some samples of both styles, a description of their most noticeable weaknesses, and the general strategy for correcting those weaknesses.

### *The Bubble Writer*

*out and I really love to be a*

*is getting so big.*

*One more thing. I have this dog named misty who thinks she*

Most modern writing styles promote the rounded, Garland effect in handwriting, but overemphasis of this form results in the Bubble writer style. As you may have already guessed, this style of handwriting is quite prevalent among teenage girls. If it appears in your writing, or in the writing of someone you know, either you or that person may be in that age group—or wish that you were. Just as bubbles float delicately upward and shimmer within themselves, a Bubble writer seems to be floating along in a self-involved little world. The excessive airy roundness of Bubble writing lends an impression of superficial form and little content.

If you qualify as a Bubble writer, you'll benefit by adding strength to your handwriting. A little extra practice of the easy non-letter–form exercises described in Part Two—such as Downstrokes, Peaks, and Teepees and Humps—will help to structure and ground your script. You'll learn a more natural way to incorporate both Angle and Garland elements in your script and reduce the Middle Zone size of your handwriting. In time, your writing will grow stronger and more legible, and your written communication will appear more mature.

## The Passive Writer

*It was also hard to get used to things.*

*I haven't done too much, just been a housekeeper.*

Lack of style combined with weak, rounded forms reveals the predominant weakness of the Passive writer. Passive writing gives the impression of an immature and easily defeated person who knows how wonderful he or she is but is unable to make others realize it. The weak form of a Passive script also suggests that the writer is a highly compromising person, easily influenced by others.

If you feel your writing matches the Passive writer style, consider adding some "backbone" to your script. Your handwriting can improve its posture just as your body can—by strengthening the spine. In handwriting, the spine is located in the pressure of the downstrokes. By practicing the Part-Two Propellers exercise and learning to put emphasis on the downstroke, you will learn how to imbue your script style with the fortitude it currently lacks. Also consider using more angular forms and increased pen pressure to add vitality to your writing. And experiment with different ink colors to find something that feels comfortable yet is distinctive.

### Famous Garland Writers

Though excessive Garland elements in handwriting can be a problem, the Garland Style also has important positive aspects. For example, the rounded writings of the Bubble writer and the Passive writer project feelings of love and protection. In this script there are no pointed or jagged letter strokes to sting the reader's eye. Depending on the originality of the handwriting, Garland writers tend to be more social and conventional in their personal expression. Their writing tends to be circular, with a medium-to-slow speed of execution. Garland writers' thinking processes tend to be more cumulative because they think through what they are going to say so as not to hurt or offend. This thoughtful behavior sometimes gives a false impression of mental slowness. In the young teen-ager this can result in the projection of an "airhead" quality.

A higher form level of Garland writing indicates a person who shows great care and concern for his or her fellowman. You will discover that some people who are famous for their contributions to mankind have Garland formations in their handwritings. Garland writers may be found among teachers, ministers, social workers, and psychologists.

*Benedico con tutto di cuore*

*Joannes Paulus pp II*

*12. Novembre 1978.*

The handwriting of Pope John Paul II contains the cuplike formations of the Garland. His signature, which essentially is a written public image, conveys feelings of care and love.

*Andrew Carnegie*

Billionaire industrialist Andrew Carnegie was well known for his philanthropic efforts. His signature mirrors his self-confidence, but also demonstrates the Garland formations that reflect his generosity.

*Spread the fragrance of Love every where you go*
*God bless you.*
*Le Teresa me*

Another famous altruistic personality is Mother Teresa of Calcutta. Her firm Garland strokes show her devotion to her work and her calm, organized way of handling her commitment to the poor and dispossessed. Notice the heartlike formation in the word *love,* which gives further evidence of her motivation to help others.

Before hurrying to change what you might feel is a weak script, consider carefully what you have learned about noted Garland writers, and see if their example highlights one of your personal goals or characteristics. You would not want to mask the loving and giving nature demonstrated in your handwriting if that is an important part of who you are. The best style for you is not what might look right to someone else, but what feels right to *you.*

## ARCADES: THE CREATIVE WRITER

Arcade writing is characterized by arched formations that cover letter forms or elaborate the beginning and ending strokes of words. If your writing sample shows excessive use of elongated, rounded strokes, your style may put you into one of two general categories: the Umbrella writer and the Guard-Up writer. Here are some samples of both styles, a description of their most noticeable weaknesses, and the general strategy for correcting those weaknesses.

### The Umbrella Writer

Umbrella writing looks like it is waiting for the world to rain on it. This style contains many convex forms that give a protected appearance to the writing. The use of unnecessary elaborations makes the writing look overembellished and difficult to read.

If you feel that you are an Umbrella writer, you may want to consider eliminating some of those tedious arched forms found in your script. The basic zone exercises in Part Two are just the thing for you. They promote simplicity in your initial and final letter-form strokes. Balancing your Arcade Style with Garland elements will project creativity and sociability to your reader.

## *The Guard-Up Writer*

*If you selected this form, you are aggressively motivated.*

*All good things come to those*

*vironment is one which lacks a cooperative spirit.*

When arcaded forms are more vertical than horizontal, the umbrella becomes a shield. Multiple shield formations identify the Guard-Up writer, a person who seems to need protection from unseen forces. The extra curves throughout the writing add an embellished and protected look to the script.

If your writing puts you in the Guard-Up category, your communication will benefit by your letting down the protective shield surrounding your script. Pay special attention to the zone exercises in Part Two and bring simplicity to your writing by eliminating elaborated ending strokes. As a result, your writing will appear more open and obliging.

## Famous Arcade Writers

The Arcade Style is less common in everyday scripts. Nevertheless, many people celebrated for their artistic and creative contributions tend to have an abundance of Arcades in their writing.

When Arcade writing has well-defined form and shading, the Arcade becomes a complimentary addition to the handwriting. Arcade writers may be found among painters, actors, designers, and inventors.

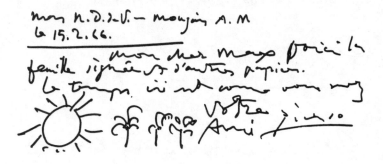

Among the varied forms in Picasso's doodles are many Arcades, the sign of an inwardly strong individualist.

The creative printscript of Thomas Edison displays Arcade forms that assert his bold ingenuity and genius. His signature especially demonstrates an umbrellalike quality that perhaps was his graphic shelter from negative criticism. The power and strength of these Arcades express his mental prowess and visionary striving.

## ANGLES: THE ANALYTICAL WRITER

Angle writing emphasizes pointed elements; letters and their connectives that normally are rounded have a pronounced angular shape. If your handwriting sample is excessively angular, your style may mark you as either a Picket-Fence writer or a Prickly Pear. Here are some samples of both styles, a description of their most noticeable weaknesses, and the general strategy for correcting those weaknesses.

### *The Picket-Fence Writer*

In these examples, notice the many angles in letter forms that are normally rounded. The upper and lower loops in the letters *d, f, g, h,* and *y* are sometimes pointed or triangular. Angled connectives between the letters *m* and *n* appear as though they are jabbing into the baseline or piercing through the Upper Zone area like a picket fence. The writing has a stiff, jagged look and marches across the page in a regimented and unbending fashion, and says as much about the writer.

If you have a Picket Fence style, relaxing the form of your script with more openness and fluidity is recommended. You'll benefit from paying extra attention to those exercises in Part Two that help you soften connective forms and emphasize roundedness and rightward movement. You'll discover that opening and rounding the Upper and Lower Zone loops in your script will lessen its rigidity.

### The Prickly Pear

*[handwriting sample]*

The unnecessary angular tics, hooks, checkmarks, and burrs that appear throughout the Prickly Pear style give readers the unpleasant impression that they would prick their finger on the writing if they had to touch it. It may be legible, but the pointy protrusions extending from various letters give it the foreboding, unfriendly look of a barbed-wire fence. Anger works as the motivator in this style, and is what it frequently communicates to the reader.

Is there a Prickly Pear quality to your script? If so, your pen crashes into the paper with such force that it bounces up and down again to form tics throughout your writing. Balance and control exercises in Part Two will help you develop smoother movement and calm your writing style.

### Famous Angled Writers

An Angle Style is frequently used by writers with an investigative personality, such as scientists and scholars. Their writing tends to be sharp, quick, and, at times, illegible due to the high speed with which they write. Their minds work faster than their motor skills as they document information for their own uses, creating scripts not necessarily to be read by others.

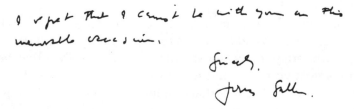

The handwriting of Dr. Jonas Salk, inventor of the polio vaccine, projects the investigative, analytical qualities consistent with the detailed, precise work he does.

> " Well, spring isn't everything, is it, Ernie? There is a lot to be said for Autumn. That's got beauty, too. And Winter — if you're together." *(Ah, Wilderness!)*
>
> Eugene O'Neill
> Jan. 1941

The handwriting of playwright Eugene O'Neill shows strength and indominability.


## THREAD: THE DIPLOMATIC WRITER

Thread writing contains many threadlike formations and diminutive letters within words that cause a breakdown in style and legibility. If you see "thread" in your writing, you may be a Squiggler or a Sidewinder. Here are samples of both styles, a description of their weaknesses, and suggestions for overcoming these tendencies.

*The Squiggler*

> The little red fox
> jumped over the fence.
> We're painting the roses red
> Alas Alas
>
> and I have been exceptionally happy

Squigglers seek the shortest distance between two points, producing handwriting that is a threaded line of unreadable letters. Squigglers' life-styles may be interesting and challenging, but also rushed and hurried. Their writing demonstrates this pace. Daily pressures and the tendency to run ahead of themselves cause both mental and physical stress that squeezes their writing into indistinguishable squiggles. They have little time to communicate, and their handwriting shows it.

Many writers seem to qualify for this category. If you are a Squiggler, focus more keenly on detailed letter forms, and temper the flow of your writing. Middle Zone exercises in Part Two will help you, since this is where major Squiggler illegibilities occur. Added rhythm and consistency gained from the balance and control exercises will make your writing more legible and calm. But most important is to take a deep breath before you write and slow down as you do it.

### The Sidewinder

This style is the result of excessive speed. The script is like a moving target—one not easy to pin down. The high-velocity letters "melt down" into indistinguishable scribbles and sinuous, wavy lines. The primary difference between a Squiggler and a Sidewinder is the degree of compression in the threaded form.

If your writing makes you a candidate for the Sidewinder category, you will benefit from paying special attention to all zone exercises in Part Two as well as to the balance and control exercises, which will help you define your final letter forms more clearly. By retaining simplicity of strokes but adding structure to your letter forms, you will be able to maintain a writing pace that is comfortable for you and still produce legible writing.

## Famous Thread Writers

The Thread Style of writing gives the impression of a hurried, evasive personality. Because speed is the main culprit, in this category we again find doctors and those with occupations or life-styles that require a quick shuffle and adept sidestepping. The twists and turns Thread Style writers add to their writing convey the message that the writers are busy, elusive, and sometimes even manipulative. Thread writers tend to be enterprising types who possess strong, persuasive verbal skills and a knack for making things happen.

Thread handwriting also gives the impression of diplomacy, but when slightly deteriorated it can connote evasiveness in the writer. When the writing becomes totally illegible, the reader may feel he or she is being deceived because the message appears hasty and unclear. Thread writers are frequently found among politicians, salespersons, lawyers, and heads of industry.

The squiggles above belong to Samuel Clemens, a.k.a. Mark Twain. He truly was a creative type, and his handwriting conveys his ability to tell tall tales and turn a phrase. One can almost sense from his rambling scrawl that he had a way of making the moments of everyday life enthralling.

Though the thread has made the above signature unreadable, this mode of self-expression is essential to the personality of this writer. The signature belongs to former Secretary of State Henry Kissinger.

## FINDING YOUR STYLE

Hold your writing sample next to the various handwriting examples in this chapter. Do any of them match your writing? Is your writing more of a combination of these styles? Do you like your style? Are there some elements you dislike and would like to change? Remember, there is no "right" way for your handwriting to look, since you have the choice of deciding what style elements are adding to or detracting from the appearance of your script.

Are you more comfortable with printing? If you are willing to print clearly and legibly, hats off to you. You are probably trying to communicate clearly and may feel that your cursive writing doesn't measure up to acceptable standards. But be aware that choosing to print limits your opportunity for natural self-expression in handwriting. Your occupation may even have influenced your choice to print. If you are an architect, drafter, or mechanical engineer you may have adopted the print script popular within your profession, though there are times when the cursive style would suit you better. If you now wish to acquire this writing style, all the exercises in this book should prove helpful to you.

Do you experience any physical discomfort when writing? If your hand cramps up or your back begins to ache, you should pay special attention to the discussions of seating position and pen grip in Part Two. By adding musical accompaniment and practicing the warm-up exercises in Part Two, you can alleviate some of your writing discomfort.

And finally, with the knowledge you now possess about this self-expressive act, you can become your own investigative analyst when chancing upon the handwriting of famous people. Ask yourself how their writing fits in with what you know of their overall talents and personality. You may be surprised at how differently you now look at handwriting and how much more aware you are of this form of self-expression.

Consider your own handwriting. If you are unhappy in your present vocation, maybe your handwriting is one more tool that can help you discover your inner goals and determine whether you are utilizing your finest talents.

PART

## 30 Days to Better Handwriting

# CHAPTER 5

*Before You Begin:*
*Understanding Movement,*
*Space, and Form*

$A$S YOU BEGIN  the second part of this book, your goal will be to develop a more simplified, rhythmical, and balanced handwriting through form drawing. By understanding writing movement, the spacing it requires, and the shape it must take to be legible, you will witness an almost immediate improvement in your script. Your aim need not be toward beautiful or calligraphic handwriting. Your main goal will be to make your writing more legible within the boundaries of your talents and innate abilities.

## THE EXERCISE CONCEPT

In this handwriting-improvement program, you will not be asked to practice the repetitious letter-form drills you may remember from your school days. The letters of the alphabet are actually composites of various kinds of basic forms or shapes in different configurations. The exercise program begins with experimentation with these various non-letter forms. The non-letter–form exercises build sequentially on one another. The forms are simple and flowing, and allow you to concentrate only on the qualities of movement, space, and form, without the interference of trying to render perfect letter symbols. During the early stages of the program, before-and-after handwriting samples at each practice session are all that is required as far as actual writing practice.

Your exercise routine will consist first of two-handed warm-up exercises to stimulate right/left-brain integration. Your breathing will also be a focal point of these exercises. By concentrating on a rhythmic in-and-out pattern, you will be able to incorporate this same pattern into your handwriting without even thinking about it.

This will be followed by selected form-drawing exercises for each zone of writing; you will be adding new exercises as you progress. At about the third week of practice, you will be ready to perform the balance and control exercises, which further integrate the two hemispheres of the brain and strengthen perceptual skills. Your final goal will be to incorporate the form drawings into the intricate symbols that constitute our cursive alphabet.

The non-letter–form exercises apply uniquely to each of the three zones of handwriting described in chapter 3. Certain exercises will be emphasized, based on your specific writing style. Be sure you understand the concepts of Garland, Arcade, Angle, and Thread Styles, both in writing and as connective forms. You also will need to determine whether any particular zone of your writing is contributing to illegibility more than others. You will then want to focus on the exercises for that zone. If it seems that no one zone contributes inordinately to the problem, simply do all the exercises in sequence; each one helps to reinforce your handwriting in some way.

*Your exercise environment.* Like all fine craftsmen, you will need certain tools to assist you with the handwriting-movement exercises. No great expense is necessary, since you may already have the essential materials needed for practice.

Ideally, you would first practice the exercises using chalk on a large chalkboard. The board could be wall-mounted and at least four feet by six feet to provide maximum range of movement, although a two-by-three-foot board would also work. These boards are available at most office-supply centers or toy stores. If a chalkboard is not available, you may use butcher paper taped to a wall or affixed to the top of your writing table with masking tape.

You will eventually be practicing on 8½-by-11-inch plain paper, using a ball-point pen. Keep a ream of typing paper and several smooth-flowing, reliable pens on hand. It's important to have your supplies readily available, in an area where you can work undisturbed and with concentration. Searching for writing materials or dealing with an inadequate work space will hinder your efforts.

*Musical accompaniment.* Your handwriting may be unattractive because it lacks rhythm and flow in the actual letter strokes. A way to subconsciously add rhythm to your writing is to perform your exercises to music. Classical pieces are preferable because of their melodic timing and unobtrusive sound. Selections from the works of Beethoven, Johann Strauss, and Bach are especially recommended to insure rhythm and consistency. However, modern selections that have a calming and rhythmic beat can serve you just as well. In any case, your handwriting equipment may now include a tape recorder and/or radio.

*Time commitment.* The first two weeks you devote to handwriting improvement will be crucial to your success. The good news is that your exercises will not require a great deal of time each day.

I suggest you practice all of the exercises designated for a certain phase in order to become comfortable with them. Then, once you have discovered which exercises are best for you, a time commitment of fifteen minutes a day is sufficient. Choose a time when you are most alert and not likely to be interrupted. Collecting before-and-after handwriting samples will help you check your progress. I suggest dating your samples so that you can keep them in chronological order.

*Steps.* The following steps are suggested for the ideal practice situation.

1. Do the warm-up exercises before each practice session.
2. Study each form drawing and write it in the air with the index finger of your natural writing hand. Closely follow your hand movement with your eyes to reinforce eye/hand coordination. (If you are working with young children, I suggest that you have them *walk* the form, and, if necessary, make a large chalk outline for them to follow. Once the walking exercise is completed, follow this by having them draw the form in the air. Also, have children use number-two pencils instead of pens.)
3. Practice the form drawing on the top of your desk or table, again using the index finger of your natural writing hand.

4. Practice the form on a chalkboard (if available) with an appropriate musical accompaniment, one that facilitates the rhythm and consistency of the form and complements your writing speed.

5. Draw the form on unlined paper while maintaining as straight a writing line as possible. If baseline control is a serious problem for you, design a page that gives you initial guidance but then slowly diminishes the extent of that help. For example:

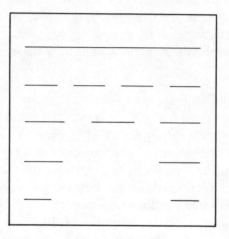

6. To make the writing exercises a twofold reward, write an affirmation when making your before-and-after writing samples. An affirmation is a positive statement that helps increase confidence and self-esteem. For example: "Every day in every way my handwriting is getting better and better." Alter these statements from time to time to avoid boredom, to practice different letter forms, and to give yourself a new "shot in the arm."

As stated, the above steps are suggested for the ideal situation, especially if you are working with children. Adults may prefer to practice on the chalkboard or butcher paper and proceed to unlined sheets of paper, though use of all the recommended steps will give you full advantage of this approach.

*An exercise chart.* To get you started and help you manage your time effectively, the following chart is offered. Keep in mind that every writer has different needs and may have to focus on specific exercises. Progress through the exercises at your own rate. The chart is merely an aid in helping you define your improvement goals as clearly and specifically as possible. Note that it does not include time for your before-and-after writing samples. To avoid illegibilities caused by speed, these writing samples should be done at a moderate pace.

### Exercise Time Chart

| Exercise Time (Minutes) | Week 1 | Week 2 | Week 3 | Week 4 |
|---|---|---|---|---|
| **Activity** | | | | |
| Warm-up exercises (develop movement and space skills) | 7 | 3 | 2 | 1 |
| Zonal exercises (develop form skills) | 8 | 8 | 5 | 5 |
| Balance and control exercises (integrate movement, space, and form) | — | — | 6 | 5 |
| Letter exercises (apply form drawings to letter forms) | — | 4 | 2 | 4 |

## THE MECHANICS OF WRITING

*Pen grip.* Each time you take pen in hand, remember that how you hold the pen will influence how well you are able to transfer writing forms to paper. Studies show that there are three basic grips and two basic hand positions commonly used by writers. The most common are the three-point and two-point grips, using, respectively, the index and middle finger with the thumb, and the index finger and thumb. The third is the lateral grip, with the thumb placed over the index finger.

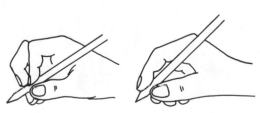 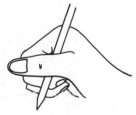

*Three-point*      *Two-point*      *Lateral*

The pen grip is an integral component of the handwriting process and may be the first clue to the cause of your handwriting problems. The two-point grip, between the index finger and the thumb, is recommended here. Only a mild amount of grip pressure is necessary in order to hold the instrument in place. The pen usually rests comfortably just below the first knuckle of the middle finger, cradled between the thumb and index finger. Preferably the index finger has a rounded arch to it, and not a caved-in appearance. The writing instrument should be held about one inch above its point. When writing, use whole-arm movements and not just an up-and-down finger motion. "Finger writing" and tight pen grip are major causes of writing fatigue.

If your pen hold does not resemble one of the three most common examples, a physical or learning problem may be the cause. Or you may be using your own hit-or-miss adaptation due to lack of instruction. If so, I suggest that you try to employ the two-point grip illustrated below, especially if your writing lacks rhythm and balance.

*Left-handed writers*

*Right-handed Writers*

*Seating position.* The best seating position advice for handwriting is the traditional "Sit up straight, with both feet flat on the floor." You probably are familiar with this position.

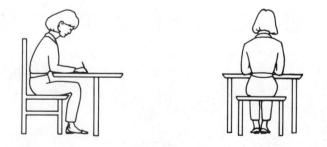

Sit firmly on the seat, with knees a little higher than hips, feet resting flat on the floor, and the spine slightly curved. Ideally, the height of the desk allows your writing arm to be close to your side without pushing up your shoulder.

*Hand position.* Use your nonwriting hand to hold the paper steady. If you are right-handed, tilt the paper to the left; if you are left-handed, tilt the paper to the right. The illustration below provides an overhead view of the correct paper and hand position for both left- and right-handed writers.

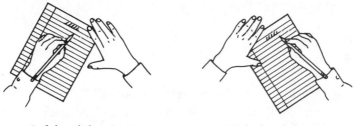

*Left-handed writers*          *Right-handed writers*

*Pressure.* In discussing pen pressure earlier, we focused solely on the concept of primary pressure. Primary pressure is the force applied when pen meets paper. Its importance lies in the proper rhythm and shading in the up-and-down flow of the handwriting.

In handwriting, the message is evident in the pressure of the downstroke. If downward pressure is weak or displaced, the writing lacks body and shading, making it difficult to read.

For example, pressure in the upstroke here does not make the message clear:

Pressure in the downstroke, though, allows the message to reveal itself:

The Downstrokes exercise in chapter 6 will help you reinforce primary pressure and make your message clear.

Another type of pressure evident in the execution of writing is secondary pressure, which is caused by the pressure you apply when holding your writing instrument. Tight grip pressure will cause your hand to tire easily and restrict the flow of your writing. Excessive secondary pressure is avoided when the first knuckle of your index finger is curved upward and not bent in when holding the pen. Minimal finger movement is desirable during writing, since ideally your forearm provides the movement as the edge of your hand glides across the page. If the intensity of either your primary or secondary pressure inhibits your writing flow, lighten up!

## GUIDING PRINCIPLES

As you progress through the exercises, you will become more aware of how these simple form drawings ultimately prepare you for the fluent writing of actual letter forms. By concentrating on the qualities of movement, space, and form in the drawings, you will gradually incorporate these features into your natural handwriting process. In this way you will have modified your preconscious approach to handwriting, enhanced your actual writing skills, and changed your basic handwriting patterns. More important, the method will prove easy, nonthreatening, and enjoyable.

Once you have mastered the movement, space, and form of the drawings, three new concepts will be applied to your specific letter forms: simplicity, rhythm, and balance.

*Simplicity.* As Henry David Thoreau cautioned, "our life is frittered away by detail . . . simplify, simplify." The same holds true for handwriting. Simplicity in handwriting is achieved by eliminating unnecessary elaborations without sacrificing clear form. This can be done by decreasing or omitting long beginning and ending strokes on letters, by printing capital letters, and by avoiding what graphologists term "ballooning" on the upper and lower loops. Simplified script gets the message across without being pretentious or overbearing.

*Rhythm.* I'm certain that you already understand the concept of rhythm in music. Good music produces a desire to move your body in time with the tune. Good handwriting also requires a sense of rhythm and tempo. Your writing should be pleasing to the eye, and your body should be physically balanced during the process of writing. When you were writing the practice sentence in chapter 4, did you find the word *communicate* difficult to write? The *mm* combination always presents a challenge: each of the downstrokes of the *m*s requires a cadence to keep them from melding together.

Cadence is the rhythmical pattern of the writing stroke as it returns to the baseline, but it is only one factor necessary to achieve rhythm in your handwriting. Other factors include a straight baseline, shading in the writing, and good picture value. The evenness of the baseline is easy to evaluate, especially if you did your sample on unlined paper. By drawing a straight penciled line under your writing, you can see how well each letter touches the imaginary baseline you established. Shading appears in the light upstroke and darker downstroke of each letter. Balanced and consistent shading add to the picture value of the writing—that is, its overall appearance. Does your sample look like something you would be willing to frame and display, or does it look like something you would like to hide in the closet? Writing that contains a fine balance of rhythm, shading, and picture value has a pleasing appearance. The reader senses that the writer valued the importance of communicating with him or her.

*Balance.* A certain amount of predictability in life makes life easier to bear and lessens stress and strain. The same is true of handwriting, especially from the reader's point of view.

Balance in handwriting means that the slant, pressure, and letter forms of the writing remain consistent. A consistent slant throughout your writing, moderate in degree, is desirable. Pressure should be consistent and most evident in the downstroke. Refrain from using several different forms of any one letter; choose the form you like the most, and stick with it. Your Upper Zone and Lower Zone letters promote the highest picture value when balanced in shape and size. Changes in slant and letter form will only make your writing that much more difficult to decipher. Remember: consistency in your writing gives the reader the impression that you are equally consistent in your behavior.

Simplicity, rhythm, and balance in writing are challenging goals that cannot be accomplished overnight. However, grasping the importance of their presence is already a giant step toward improvement.

Try not to become frustrated or defeated. Change takes time, especially when you are changing a motor skill you have practiced most of your life.

When doing the exercises, think positive. These exercises are fun and effective, and allow you to be in control. Get yourself motivated with a pre-exercise sample that says, "Every day, in every way, my handwriting is getting better."

CHAPTER *6*

# Exploring Movement, Space, and Form in Your Handwriting

*W*HAT A WONDERFUL, enlightening experience it is to discover that the games and songs presented in childhood had a twofold purpose. As youngsters we responded to games like hopscotch and to songs like "Eentsy Weentsy Spider" only because they were fun. But they served another purpose: the tossing and hopping required in hopscotch reinforced physical coordination; and the finger movements of "Eentsy Weentsy Spider" enhanced visual/motor integration.

After kindergarten, we are asked to put aside much of the singing, dancing, and drawing in exchange for more serious learning exercises. And though educators ardently profess that learning can be fun, little joy is to be found in the memorization and repetition that they ask of us. In this chapter you will be reintroduced to enjoyable learning through coordination games and exercises.

**Purpose:** The exercises in this chapter are designed to develop better coordination in the physical act of handwriting and to stimulate right/ left-brain functions.

**Method:** You will use both your right and left hands simultaneously, drawing forms to achieve total body involvement and whole-brain thinking.

**Duration:** These exercises are essential as warm-ups to your everyday practice and should be continued throughout your exercise sessions.

**Terms to Remember:**
Brainwriting          Right Brain          Left Brain

**Guiding Principles:** Physical coordination of fine motor skills and balance in both the right and left hemispheres of the brain lead to balance in the handwriting.


## *Handwriting is Brainwriting*

Where does your handwriting really originate? The letters of the alphabet are simply stored bits of information that you have learned to associate with sound in order to form words. When you wish to put these words on paper, the most convenient method is to use your normal writing hand. But what happens if there is injury to or loss of the hand? This question was presented by Wilhelm Preyer, a German physiologist, who in 1895 coined the word *brainwriting.* He observed that similar writing patterns were produced by the use of different body members such as the right hand, the left hand, the mouth, and the foot. More recently, Robert Saudek reported in his classic work *Experiments with Handwriting* that "the expression of handwriting remains basically unchanged whether the writing is executed with the right hand or with the left hand, and even with the mouth or with the toes." The impulses from the brain are what really constitute handwriting and contribute to making each person's writing unique.

Handwriting has the distinction of being an art form as well as a means of communication. Why is it an art form? Simply stated, in handwriting the letter forms are copied from a model, just as a bowl of fruit serves as a model for a still-life painting. All artists (and writers) have their own perception of what each form should look like. Visit any life-drawing class and you will find as many variations in the reproduction of the model as there are students in the class. The same diversity in forms is manifest when students are first introduced to the cursive alphabet. Just as a bowl of fruit provides reference for artists, the letter symbols provide models for writers.

In this perspective the act of handwriting can be considered to have much in common with many other artistically expressive actions, particularly drawing, painting, and sculpting. All of these involve the integration of complex perceptual and physiological functions in the brain. One of the most elegant and illuminating descriptions of that process can be found in *Drawing on the Right Side of the Brain,* the classic instructional text on drawing by Betty Edwards.

Based on research into brain function, Edwards' book describes the different ways that the right and left hemispheres of the human brain interpret and process information, and how those separate processes can be integrated to improve artistic skill.

In general terms, research has shown that the left hemisphere of the brain processes information in what is called a "verbal, analytic" style, whereas the right hemisphere specializes in a "spatial, global" type of processing. Though the two hemispheres differ in their processing and retrieval of information, they are not separate entities. A bridge—a bundle of nerve fibers known as the corpus callosum—connects the two hemispheres of the brain. Thus, neither side of the brain has total dominance over our actions.

In *Drawing on the Right Side of the Brain,* Betty Edwards tells us:

> In all kinds of activities, the brain uses both hemispheres, perhaps at times with the halves alternating in "leading," perhaps at times each carrying an equal share of a task.

Right- and left-brain functions are not always ideally balanced, however. Language and time-related skills are usually located in the left hemisphere; because our culture is so oriented to verbal communication and time relationships, we often function in a "left mode" style of cognition, which can limit our abilities in creative actions like drawing and handwriting. As the title of Dr. Edwards' book implies, "right-mode" cognition can result in perceptual breakthroughs that enhance artistic skill. Her book demonstrates how you can achieve that breakthrough and learn to use it when it is useful to do so—in effect, consciously balancing your brain functions.

### Influence of the Brain on Handedness

Why are you right-handed? Or left-handed? The brain plays an important part in determining this. In general, the right hemisphere of the brain controls the left half of the body, and the left hemisphere controls the right. The following sketch from *Drawing on the Right Side of the Brain* demonstrates the crossover connections involving the brain and handedness.

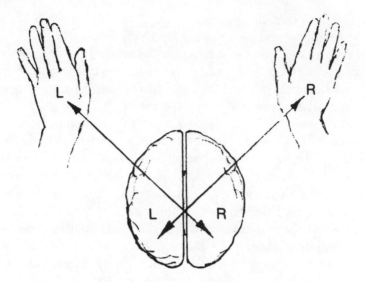

*The crossover connections of left hand to right hemisphere,
right hand to left hemisphere*

However, this does not mean all left-handers are right-brain dominant. In their book *Whole-Brain Thinking,* Jacquelyn Wonder and
Priscilla Donovan report some unique findings based on preferred
pen grip:

> In studies [conducted by Jerry Levi] of the four handwriting positions
> (normal right, normal left, hooked right and hooked left), it was found
> that left-handers who hold the pencil in a normal handwriting position and
> right-handers who use a hooked handwriting position both have primary
> speech functions in their right hemispheres. This is a disadvantage for
> language skills, since the left is most appropriate for logical, articulate
> speech. The same research showed that persons who have the normal
> right-hand style have primary language in the left hemisphere, as do
> left-handers who write with a hooked-hand position, an advantage to
> language skills.

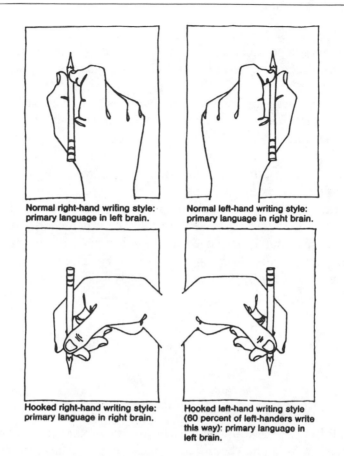

Normal right-hand writing style: primary language in left brain.

Normal left-hand writing style: primary language in right brain.

Hooked right-hand writing style: primary language in right brain.

Hooked left-hand writing style (60 percent of left-handers write this way): primary language in left brain.

Problems can develop when one side of the brain dominates the other. However, by stimulating both hemispheres at the same time, you can achieve balance in right/left-hemisphere functions. Utilizing the best of both hemispheres, you can produce a handwriting that not only communicates clearly but is pleasing to the eye.

## WARM-UP EXERCISES

### TWO WHEELS
The lack of time devoted to helping students understand the dynamics of movement, space, and form is one of the major problems in teaching handwriting. Rapid introduction of letter shapes by the teacher

creates a tendency for the student to concentrate on the intricacies of the letter and emphasizes the motor skills of only the preferred writing hand. Using such an approach leaves little preparation for rhythm and balance.

*Balance* implies a two-sided effort, with each side contributing the same amount of energy. Since handwriting is really brainwriting, stimulating both sides of the brain simultaneously will make the contribution even. Cerebral balance for this motor skill can be accomplished by using both hands during a writing-movement exercise.

The following exercise helps you achieve your own rhythm and turns writing into a whole-body experience. Both sides of the brain are stimulated, and a "crossover" or balance is achieved. Using both hands to draw the form facilitates development of the right- and left-brain hemispheres and stimulates memory. The more clearly you can remember a form, the more accurately you can reproduce it.

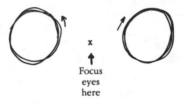

Focus
eyes
here

*The balancer*

You'll benefit the most by performing this exercise in a large format, such as on a chalkboard or butcher paper. Mark the center of your writing surface with a small *x* and focus your attention on that mark. With your nose approximately six inches from the *x,* focus your eyes directly at the center mark. You'll be making writing movements to the left and right of the *x.* Avoid checking your forms, since turning your head or eyes from side to side will interfere with the balance effect we seek.

With a piece of chalk in each hand, make outward circular movements. The large circles should be done in an up-and-away direction. The right hand circles in a clockwise direction, the left in a counterclockwise direction. The outward circular movement of the Two Wheels exercise helps achieve independent yet simultaneous movement of the two hands.

It is recommended that this exercise be done for a few seconds before each session. Make a point of achieving total body involvement when making the circles.

## LAZY EIGHT

For any physical exercise, breathing is essential to the natural flow of energy. This is also true for the exercise of handwriting. If you think of the writing upstroke as the taking in of oxygen and the downstroke as the release of oxygen, it is possible to visualize your own breathing pattern in your handwriting. Inconsistent breathing patterns will produce inconsistencies in the handwriting. Again, balance is the key, via stimulation of both brain hemispheres.

For some people, writing from one side of the paper to the other is actually a difficult process. The following exercise will help you make that movement in a free-flowing and relaxed manner.

*The breather*

The chalkboard or butcher paper is best for this exercise. First practice making just one form. Using your normal writing hand, start the form upward to the right and loop back to the left, returning to the midpoint to complete your Lazy Eight. Repeat the form several times, retracing your initial path. Focus on crossing at the midpoint. (An inability to cross the midline indicates problems in reading from left to right.)

Now practice the movement with your opposite writing hand. Once you have the form mastered, you are ready to attempt the pattern using both hands at the same time. The trick is to again focus your vision on an $x$ in the center of your writing area and concentrate only on the form and movement of the Lazy Eights. You will achieve better results when you bring your whole body into the movement, swaying with the form, to help facilitate drawing.

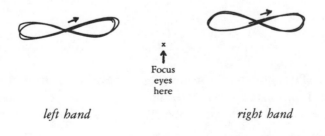

x
↑
Focus
eyes
here

*left hand*          *right hand*

If, in the beginning, this exercise proves too difficult, try drawing the forms in the air using the index fingers of each hand. Whether drawing on the board or in the air, your normal writing hand will initially perform better than the opposite hand.

## RIGHT/LEFT-BRAIN EXERCISES

By using both hands in the following exercises, you can work on achieving balance in your handwriting. Again, the best way to practice is on a wall-mounted chalkboard that provides you with ample space for movement.

*THE FOUNTAIN*

The Fountain is a way of reaching out in your writing without being concerned about space and form. With eyes straight ahead and a piece of chalk or pen in each hand, make upward spouting lines. Be sure to allow your arms to work simultaneously up and out, circling the air before making the next upward stroke. Reach as far as you can, bending your knees and stretching your arms as freely as possible to make a strong and gushing fountain.

*TRIANGLES*

Practicing Triangles adds the angles necessary to strengthen your writing and stimulates the analytical components of your brain. Beginning at the bottom of the chalkboard, make two parallel lines upward with chalk in each hand. Next, draw diagonal lines out from the center and then in again to complete the triangular forms. Repeat the forms several times, one on top of the other, without lifting the chalk from the board.

*DIAMONDS*

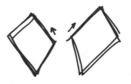

Diamonds expand upon the triangular form, adding more angles and directional changes. Beginning at the center of the chalkboard, make two diagonal lines up and then down to form the upper peak of the diamond. Complete the diamond form by mirroring this same peak on the bottom. Repeat the form several times, one on top of the other, without lifting the chalk from the board.

*DOWNSTROKES*

In handwriting, the message is evident in the downstroke. If downward pressure is weak, the writing lacks body and shading, making it difficult to read. The Downstrokes exercise, designed to strengthen the downward pressure in handwriting, insures that the writer's message is clear and legible.

Downstrokes can be performed in two ways: first, by alternating the right and left hand in a swinging motion while alternating the feet in a marching pattern. Hence, when the right hand is making the downward stroke, the left foot is off the floor, and vice versa for the left hand and right foot. This pattern is also one prescribed for brain-injured patients or for children with learning problems.

Second, the downward strokes may be drawn simultaneously with the right and left hands, beginning at the top of the chalkboard and proceeding downward in a straight line. Whole-body movement is important with this exercise: the knees must bend, and the arms need to swing up and back in a strong and rhythmical fashion.

*CROSS-STROKES*

*right hand*      *left hand*

This exercise transforms your parallel lines into crossing diagonals. It's important to remember that the lines are made outward, alternating right and left. The right hand starts on the left side and swings out beside the right hip. Then the left hand starts on the right side and swings out beside the left hip. If you have a tendency to do the opposite, you are "crossing" yourself out, and this X'ing with your arms blocks the energy necessary for you to sustain a free-flowing movement in your writing.

*FANTASY ANIMALS*

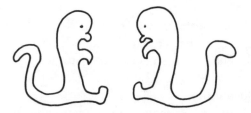

Here you have a chance to create your own forms. This is a fun exercise. It has no rules except that you must draw your creations with both hands at the same time. Play some happy, rhythmical music to accompany this exercise, and let your imagination guide you. As best you can, try to make your right and left hands do the same strokes at the same time as you allow yourself to experience free-style design.

## FINGER EXERCISES

Significant eye-and-hand coordination is required to hold the writing instrument and guide it along the writing line. If your hand does not seem to be getting the message from your brain, then you must strive to improve your dexterity. Just as a newborn baby exhibits fascination with the discovery of his or her hands, you will also be fascinated by the new awareness you develop in doing these sometimes simple, sometimes difficult finger exercises.

### TABLETOP GYMNASTICS

Lay your hands flat on the table. Take a moment to appreciate the wonder of your hands and how hard they work for you. Now get ready to send messages from your brain to your fingers and see how well you are able to respond to these commands.

First, spread the second and third finger of one hand and bring them back together. Next, spread the third and fourth finger and bring them back together, then the fourth and fifth. Practice with each hand. You will discover that the least-used fingers in writing are the ones hardest to control in this exercise. Even more challenging is doing this exercise in the air, without the feel of the table beneath your hands.

For more tabletop gymnastics, lay yours hands flat on the table once again and lift each finger, one at a time, as if you were counting them off in a line. Lift all ten digits in consecutive order, back and forth. Are you surprised when some fingers pop up out of order? That ring finger likes to be stubborn; you may be able to lift it only slightly.

### BLIND MAN'S BLUFF

Once you have mastered the lifting of each finger, close your eyes and have someone give you verbal commands to further test your sensory awareness. The caller should mix commands such as "Raise the second finger on your right hand" and "Raise the third finger on your left hand." Be aware of your concentration and brain impulses as they race to give the message to your fingers. The tabletop now becomes your ally as you use it to reinforce the location and position of each finger.

### CLIMBING THE LADDER

The alternating movements of Climbing the Ladder increase finger dexterity and right/left-brain coordination. To begin, touch the top of the thumb of one hand with the top of the index finger of the other hand—that is, right thumb with left index finger. Cross over at the top with the opposite thumb and opposite index finger. Practice this movement until it becomes smooth and quick. Now progress to the thumb and third finger of each hand, then thumb and fourth finger, and finally thumb and fifth finger. Do this exercise repeatedly until it becomes an easy, progressive movement.

### THE CROSS-OVER

Though a difficult exercise, the Cross-Over will have you laughing at your directional confusion. Begin with your hands laid flat on the table in front of you. Lift both the right and left hands at the same time and allow your forearms to cross paths, making an *x* at about chest level. Now with the thumb and index finger of your right hand, grip your left ear, and with the thumb and index finger of your left hand, hold your nose. Alternate left and right hands until you figure out exactly where these body parts are located. Notice how your level of concentration and your ability to judge distance increase. The Cross-Over challenges your left/right coordination. The flailing of arms and tendency to pinch cheeks and poke eyes make this exercise difficult to master but always entertaining.

## INTERPRETING YOUR RESULTS

The two-handed drawings and finger exercises outlined in this chapter are an enjoyable way to stimulate your motor skills and brain functions. There is no right or wrong way of doing them. But there may be an element of frustration, especially with the finger exercises, when you first practice them. Don't allow this to upset you. Instead, enjoy your fumbling and work at improving your dexterity a little at a time. At some point it will all come together and you will be amazed at your progress.

*Garland Style writers.* The two-handed drawings illustrated in this chapter are especially helpful in adding more creativity to your script if you are a Garland Style writer. The more conventional look of this writing style sometimes does not allow for artistic expression. This expression can be awakened by the right-brain stimulation of the two-handed exercises.

*Arcade Style writers.* If you are an Arcade Style writer, you may need to add more linear qualities to your handwriting, and the left-brain stimulation of the two-handed exercises could give you the balance necessary to achieve that.

*Angle Style writers.* If you are an Angle Style writer, the warm-up exercises would best serve you as a preliminary relaxation technique. The rhythmic and rounded forms of these exercises can help reduce the tension and rigidity that sometimes dominate this writing style.

*Thread Style writers.* Speed is a strong influence in your writing if you are a Thread Style writer. The slowing down necessary to perform all the exercises in this chapter should prove helpful in increasing your awareness of line quality and clear form, especially in the more geometric drawings.

Although these exercises may not seem specifically related to actual cursive handwriting, their practice is essential in fine-tuning your motor and perceptual skills. Think of them as a fun way to begin your exercise sessions. Their beneficial aspects will become increasingly evident to you as a means not only of whole-brain involvement in handwriting, but of whole-body involvement as well.

# CHAPTER 7

# Exercising Your Middle, Upper, and Lower Zones

*T*HE ACTUAL FORM-DRAWING exercises that will result in better handwriting begin in this chapter. The forms in these exercises have intentionally been given names that do not associate them with any particular letter. The goal is to stimulate your right-brain creative talents by keeping the forms simple and concrete, without left-brain symbol interpretation.

**Purpose:** Zonal form drawings provide a componentlike approach to forming the actual letters of the alphabet and promote the connective nature of cursive script.

**Method:** First read through the entire exercise section; then simply add a few exercises each day. Focus on the forms that address your own personal handwriting problems based on the results of your writing-style test. Not all forms need to be practiced by all writers. When appropriate, some forms will be referenced in relation to a particular writing style. If no reference is given with a form, then all writers will benefit from practicing that form. At first, you may draw the forms in any size that feels comfortable to you. Design some gradually reduced lined paper as discussed in chapter 5, and eventually practice on unlined paper to develop a sense of spatial control.

**Duration:** Zonal form drawings are practiced throughout your handwriting-improvement program. The optimal amount of practice for each form drawing is specified as each form is described.

**Terms to Remember:**

Middle Zone Form Drawings

Upper Zone Form Drawings

Lower Zone Form Drawings

**Guiding Principles:** The forms are merely drawings that have not yet been absorbed into your preconscious mind. Once the forms become second nature to you, they will automatically become a part of your handwriting. Thus, you will eventually improve your writing without repetition of letter forms or fear of producing less-than-perfect symbols.

## *MIDDLE ZONE FORM DRAWINGS*

Since all letters pass through the Middle Zone of cursive handwriting, it is only natural that we begin with the form drawings for this zone. The Middle Zone letters are *a, c, e, i, m, n, o, r, s, u, v, w,* and *x.* When shaping these letters, a combination of Garland and Angle forms is optimal.

*LITTLE LOOPS*

Your first Middle Zone exercise involves the creation of the rounded, open form of Little Loops. Though this exercise may seem elementary to you, it is a good relaxation technique and helps you eliminate unnecessary constriction in your writing. Constriction involves a narrowing or retracing of a loop when a fuller form is desirable. Little Loops promote fluid left-to-right movement and balanced spatial arrangement. Doing a full page of Little Loops reinforces spatial arrangement by making you aware of margins and letter and line spacing. The continual flow of the writing instrument across the page introduces you to the connected movement necessary in cursive handwriting.

Continue to practice Little Loops every day, first a full page, then three or four lines before doing the other Middle Zone forms, until their shape and flow become integrated into your handwriting.

*CUPS*

A Garland connective is taught as the primary connective form between letters in most cursive scripts. The form drawing of Cups is especially helpful for practicing this basic handwriting element.

Practice a full page of these forms, making certain that each downstroke returns to the writing line and that the form is rounded at the base. Keep the width of each cup as uniform as possible, and utilize the same spatial arrangement in lines and margins that you used for the Little Loops exercise. After your initial full page of Cups, practice three or four lines for at least the first week of your exercise schedule.

*HUMPS*

By inverting Cups, you create Humps. This form drawing facilitates cadence in your writing. Cadence is the rhythmic return to the baseline of each downstroke, which is especially noticeable in certain letters. Concentrate on keeping the downstrokes even in length, using a rounded formation at the top and a consistent width in each arch.

When beginning to practice this form, follow the same instructions as were given for the previous exercises—a full page and then a few lines.

*PEAKS*

The most common connective combination in basic cursive writing is the Garland/Angle letter connection. If you were to practice only form drawings that were soft and rounded, you might end up with Bubble Writing as described in chapter 4. Therefore, it is essential to also add strength to your writing by improving your ability to incorporate angular forms.

Peaks will help you make sudden changes of direction in your writing without loosing the cadence necessary to maintain rhythm and balance. The peak formations will subtly find their way into some of your letter forms. This connective lessens the tendency to create an overly rounded look in your handwriting, one that could be regarded as monotonous or immature.

Peaks are best done a few lines at a time. This exercise applies more to the Garland Style writer than to the Angle Style writer.

*OCEAN WAVES*

Ocean Waves are probably the most challenging of the Middle Zone form drawings. The right-left directional change of the curl in the wave invites the possibility of looping. This curl requires a leftward retracing that needs a steady hand and focused concentration.

Ocean Waves may require more practice than the other Middle Zone exercises. Don't become discouraged if you tend to loop or angle the retracing at the top of the wave; just continue along the row, applying a rightward force at the base of each wave. Concentrate on eye/hand coordination, and slow down if necessary. Staying aware of the signals your hand is receiving from the brain will increase your perception and sharpen your visual acuity.

Practice a full page of Ocean Waves at first, and be sure to include at least three or four lines throughout your form-drawing practice sessions.

*CASTLE TOPS*

Castle Tops perfectly illustrate the incorporation of both Garlands and Angles. Sharp, level mesas on each form create an impressive castle wall.

A few lines of Castle Tops are all that is necessary for your initial practice. This form will later be paired with other exercises that emphasize connections that do not return to the baseline.

*RIPPLES*

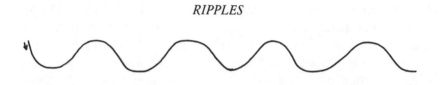

The Ripples form drawing has a calming, fluid effect on the writer. This form is much simpler than Ocean Waves, but care must be taken to avoid threading it out or losing the humplike quality of each ripple. Thread Style writers may have a tendency to do this and should make an extra effort to form the top of the Ripples distinctly. Angle Style writers should take care not to "peak" the humps. This exercise emphasizes the execution of fluid movement without the loss of form and control.

A half page of Ripples ought to familiarize you with this movement. Use it as a relaxation exercise when you feel there is too much tension in your handwriting.

## Combinations

Cursive writing is a complex task that involves the incorporation of many forms at the same time. Exercises that combine both the constriction and release of loop formations make an excellent introduction to the eventual consolidation of all the forms. Of course, such exercises require more concentration and, again, eye-hand coordination, but the rhythm and accuracy that result are well worth the effort.

*LOOPS AND CUPS*

The Loops and Cups combination helps you apply both constriction and expansion in your handwriting. With this exercise you will get a feel for the necessary concentration that a change of form demands.

Once this form drawing is added to your exercise session, you need not practice Cups and Little Loops by themselves anymore. You have graduated to more sophisticated forms. A full page of Loops and Cups would be best for initial practice, again checking margins and spacing. Reduce this to a few lines once you feel you have mastered the rhythm of constriction and release involved in this form drawing.

### HUMPS AND CUPS

The Humps and Cups combination emphasizes accuracy and precision of line placement. First make a line of Humps, and then center the Cups as precisely as possible within the Humps. Keep the spacing consistent between each arch. The control and spatial arrangement you practice in this combination will reinforce the same qualities in your handwriting.

Initially perform a half page to a full page of this form, and continue its practice if you have difficulty in keeping a straight baseline in your before-and-after writing samples.

### CUPS AND CASTLE TOPS

This exercise combines the Garland/Angle forms that are the most common primary and secondary connectives between letters. Alternating Cups and Castle Tops helps you practice the difficult waistline connector, a connective that does not return to the baseline of writing.

Practice a full page of this form. At this point, you may eliminate the practice of Cups and Castle Tops as single-form drawings. Continue with a few lines of this form each time you practice your Middle Zone exercises.

*DOUBLE WAVES*

Once you feel you have mastered the unique flow of Ocean Waves, you are ready to challenge yourself with this combined form, which utilizes the same form within itself. The Double Waves exercise reinforces spacing and develops a rhythm for the right-to-left flow of this form.

Draw a line of Ocean Waves, and then, along the same baseline, interweave another row of waves. This exercise will encourage you to make a strong rightward thrust after each wave in order to provide space for the interwoven forms. A full page is recommended for initial practice, followed by at least three or four lines at each exercise session.

## UPPER ZONE FORM DRAWINGS

The upward extensions of cursive script require a special combination of up-and-down pen pressure. For the proper shading and emphasis, increased pressure should occur in the downstroke of the loop. It is also imperative that the exercises for the Upper Zone letters be paired with some Middle Zone form drawings, since this is the natural style of cursive writing. The Upper Zone letters include *b, d, h, k, l, t,* and the upper extension of the trizonal letter *f.*

*LITTLE LOOPS AND BIG LOOPS*

This exercise is a fundamental drill that encourages you to concentrate but allows you freedom of movement within its smooth, rounded forms. You will develop the rhythm necessary to make zonal changes in your writing without having to concern yourself with too many form changes.

When you are ready to tackle a page of these forms, use the same spatial awareness you applied when practicing Little Loops. For a greater challenge, try using different combinations of Big Loops and Little Loops—for example, one Little Loop and two Big Loops. You'll be surprised at how often you are tempted to stay in the Middle Zone.

Example:

*elle elle elle*

An initial full page of practice followed by a few lines during each session will satisfy both the Little Loop and Big Loop exercise requirements. Understand that you really haven't stopped practicing any particular form. You have instead combined forms, building on your form-drawing skills, which in turn will enhance your handwriting capabilities.

### BIG LOOPS AND CASTLE TOPS

*bbbbbbbbbb*

This exercise emphasizes the Garland/Angle combination in its pairing of Big Loops with Castle Tops. The troublesome above-baseline connector is presented, along with the combined forms and zonal changes that are common in cursive handwriting.

Practice a full page when first learning this form drawing, and then reduce your practice to three or four lines. Building your skills with combined forms prepares you for the complex combination of all the forms that constitutes cursive handwriting.

### SWINGING BRIDGE

*ttt ttt ttt*

Now that you are accustomed to making full, open loops after practicing Big Loops, focus on retracing the up-and-down strokes that formed them. The Swinging Bridge exercise provides practice for some Upper Zone forms that are best not made with open loops. Be sure to draw the bridge "cable" about three-quarters of the way up, using a strong and straight rightward stroke.

Practice a full page of Swinging Bridges the first time you perform this form drawing. Thereafter, a few lines will suffice. Strong horizontal carry-through on the crossbar is especially recommended if your writing-style sample showed evidence of light pressure and weak letter forms.

*PROPELLERS*

The Propellers form drawing introduces the upper-loop–lower-loop combination that occurs in some cursively written words. When practicing this form, be sure to use a straight downward stroke after completing the top loop. Strive for erect forms and for balance in the form and size of the loops.

A full page of Propellers is highly recommended each time this form is practiced. Propellers also prove to be an excellent relaxation exercise and should be practiced by Angle Style writers in particular.

## LOWER ZONE FORM DRAWINGS

Just as the upward extensions of cursive script require a special application of writing pressure, so do the lower extensions. Again, the downstroke gets the most pressure. With the Lower Zone forms, this stroke comes first, followed by released pressure in the upstroke of the loop as it returns to the baseline. Lower Zone exercises will also be paired with Middle Zone form drawings, since this is the natural flow in cursive handwriting. Open, rounded loops followed by a definite return to the baseline should be your goal when doing these exercises.

The Lower Zone letters include *g, j, p, q, y, z,* and the lower extension of the trizonal letter *f.*

*UPSIDE-DOWN LITTLE LOOPS AND BIG LOOPS*

As you do this exercise, feel how the Lower Zone loops exit the Middle Zone with a definite downward plunge. It is important to develop a confident downward departure from the baseline. Concentrate on the movement through the zones, and keep your loops open and rounded.

Practice a full page of this form drawing until you feel comfortable with the shading, spacing, and consistency of your loops. Once you have achieved this, three to four lines of this combination are all that is necessary.

*PROPELLERS*

This Upper Zone exercise proves useful for Lower Zone letters as well. For Lower Zone forms, place special emphasis on the downstroke. Remember to make a straight spine and to balance the loops at both ends.

*POUCHES*

This form drawing helps combat the contrariness of the lower loops appearing in some cursive letters. If these tend to give you trouble in your handwriting, practice pouches at least a few times.

## *INTERPRETING YOUR RESULTS*

As you practice these form drawings, you will become your own instructor and judge. Here are some important things to look for in your work. First, always check elements of arrangement as discussed in chapter 3. After completing a page of forms, hold your paper at arm's length to see if the lines are straight and if there is consistent spacing between each loop or form and each consecutive line. Check margins to see if they are even on both sides of the paper.

Vision problems and learning disabilities can make it difficult for a writer to maintain a continual writing flow without drooping the lines or constricting the loops. Tension and stress may add peaks and angles to rounded forms, making them appear rigid. So although the fundamental form and movement of Little Loops may appear easy to you, the same may not hold true for everyone. Look at the problems some writers experienced:

*Loops made by a fourteen-year-old dysgraphic boy with vision problems*

*Little loops made by an Iranian woman*
*unfamiliar with rounded, rightward forms*

In making any type of zonal loop, *balance* and *simplicity* must be the bywords. Ballooning of the loops only distracts the eye and clutters the page. Be aware of this when doing Little Loop–Big Loop combinations for both the Upper and Lower Zone form drawings. Propellers are a good gauge for checking whether you are making one zone fuller than the other.

In performing form drawings such as Humps and Cups and the Swinging Bridge, avoid looping between each form. Keeping the forms rounded on the top or bottom and maintaining consistent size and a straight baseline may require the use of a lined page at first.

The complex movement of the Ocean Waves form drawing may cause you some problems when the retracing of the curl is not done properly. Inability to retrace correctly can cause illegibility in the many letters that the Ocean Wave helps to form. The Ocean Wave, when combined with upper and lower extensions, forms letters of all three zones; it also appears in an inverted position in some letters.

Often, due to the right/left flow of the Ocean Wave, there exists the tendency (especially in children's writing) to take the easy way around with this form.

*Example of the all-the-way-around form found in some handwritings*

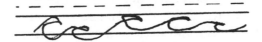

*Example of an eleven-year-old boy's tendency to loop the curl when drawing Ocean Waves*

*Ocean Waves drawn by an elderly Korean man, showing a resistant directional pull as though the waves are breaking into the wind*

You can now see that form drawing provides a componentlike approach to cursive handwriting. The combination exercises will feel easier to you after you master the individual form drawings. You will begin to get a sense for the directional and form changes that make handwriting a sometimes difficult task.

# CHAPTER 8

## *Exploring Balance and Control*

$A$T THIS POINT, you have been introduced to all the form drawings necessary to make every letter of the alphabet. Still, good form constitutes only one ingredient of beautiful handwriting. In this chapter you will learn the balance and control necessary to gracefully combine form with space and movement. You will do some conceptual blockbusting, looking beyond mere letter forms and exploring the dynamics of spatial awareness. By expanding your handwriting skills in a more artful and creative way, you will find that you look at the design of your writing in a whole new light as you become the creator of your own special forms.

**Purpose:** Balance and control exercises provide control over space and form in handwriting and provide further integration of the functions of the right and left hemispheres of the brain.

**Method:** You will practice nonzonal form drawings that emphasize the direction and balance necessary in handwriting as well as mirror images, which develop an appreciation for visual perception and combine the symbolic and concrete aspects of handwriting.

**Duration:** Balance and control exercises are practiced in the third week of your exercise program at selected intervals during zonal-form-drawing practice.

**Terms to Remember:**

| | |
|---|---|
| Simplicity | Control |
| Rhythm | Imaginary baseline |
| Balance | |

**Guiding Principles:** Mastery of complex directional forms builds confidence in rendering legible, expressive letter forms. The concentration and focus required to perform these exercises create a balance within the body that is projected into the handwriting.

*CLOVERS*

Clovers are a way of relaxing your writing hand while still emphasizing the directional flow of cursive handwriting. To make your Clover, begin by making a Lazy Eight. Start at the center and go to the right in an upward movement, then to the left. Next make the top loop to the right and come down rightward into the bottom loop.

The rhythm of the movement is right, left, up, down. Retrace your form as many times as you like, and keep the loops as even and balanced in size as possible. This form is an excellent addition to your warm-up exercises and is best practiced regularly from this point on.

You can expand on the clover form by making the drawing more precise in line quality and distance of each loop. First make an initial clover. Then expand the clover outward three or four times, using the same right, left, up, down rhythm. The trick is to cross the center point at the same place each time and maintain the same distance between the lines in each loop. Practice this form after first doing at least two regular Clovers.

### LOOP-THE-LOOP

The Propellers exercise introduced in chapter 7 appears here in a slightly different form, one that emphasizes the balance of all three zones. It is simply a joining of Little Loops and Propellers.

Begin with a Little Loop. Proceed rightward, alternating Little Loops and Propellers. Be sure to make the Propeller downstroke straight, with balanced loops on top and bottom.

Do a full page of the Loop-the-Loop exercise your first time; afterward, do a few lines at a time as an additional warm-up exercise.

### GRADUATED LOOPS

This exercise borrows two of your earlier basic forms, the Big Loop and the Little Loop, and incorporates their right-side-up and upside-down forms.

Begin by making a Little Loop. Then make a medium-sized loop, followed by a Big Loop. Finish the form by making another medium-sized loop and then a Little Loop, keeping them the same size and shape as the first two, with the Big Loop centered between them. Next, simply invert this form to point downward.

Draw at least two rows of these forms, making sure to keep both upward and downward loops even in height, length, and width. Practice this form in each session until you feel comfortable with it.

### WISHBONES

A popular control exercise is Wishbones—or Push-Pulls, as they are sometimes called. This form is especially beneficial for initiating control in handwriting and for stimulating thinking processes.

Begin at your chosen baseline and bend the line slightly upward and to the right. Make an upward peak and then begin to retrace it, moving back down and then to the right with another rounded line. Continue across the page, keeping the forms connected and maintaining even peaks and a steady baseline.

Though this exercise is challenging, a full page of Wishbones is recommended for your first practice, followed by a few lines at each subsequent session.

*STARS*

Nothing could be easier than making straight lines. That's all that is required for this exercise. Try to keep all angles the same.

Begin by making a vertical line as the center of your Star. Follow this with a horizontal line crossing at the middle. Then draw a diagonal line from upper right to lower left. Draw the last diagonal from upper left to lower right.

Make your Stars box-shaped, with each line intersecting exactly at the midpoint. Making two lines of this form will convince you that it is not as easy as it looks. This is a fun doodle you can practice as often as you wish.

*THE MAZE*

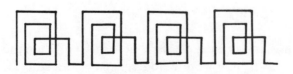

This design adds strength and control to your handwriting.

Begin with an upward vertical line, and form a box that turns within itself. Continue until you have made a third inward box. Exit horizontally to the right and then downward. Make a short horizontal line along the baseline and then upward again, repeating your box form.

When drawing the Maze, try to maintain the same distance between each line, and keep the horizontals and verticals straight. Practice three lines of this form and then continue its use, especially if your writing samples seem weak and lacking in baseline control.

*SPIRALS*

Spirals are similar to the Maze. Both emphasize all the directions involved in writing movement.

Begin your first Spiral at the left and curl inward two times, with the final curl pointing rightward. Lifting your pen, create an inner Spiral that follows the same path in reverse, with the beginning curl pointing leftward. Maintain the same distance between each line and push out toward the right, leaving room for the next exiting Spiral.

If you copy your earlier movement, you can avoid the tendency for the line to droop. The inward-curling Spiral must not reach as low as the previous exiting Spiral. The exiting line is the one that rests on your imaginary baseline.

Practice a full page of Spirals, concentrating on space and form. Continue with a few lines per day until you feel you have mastered the complexity of this form.

## MIRROR DRAWINGS

Mirror drawings involve the drawing of forms, and then the mirroring of their image as if they were being reflected in a still pond. As you do the first part of each exercise, use a left-brain approach, saying to yourself the shape each stroke should take—for example, *hump, hump, peak.* Shift to a right-brain mode when mirroring the forms by concentrating on line quality and movement, relying less on verbal cues and more on spatial arrangement. Although for the right-brain–left-brain exercises in chapter 7 you used both hands, here you will use only your normal writing hand. Your alternating verbal and nonverbal approach will be the stimulant for the two hemispheres of the brain.

The reflective nature of mirror drawings subliminally promotes the concept of relationship. When creating the first line of forms, you focus only on the image in your own mind. While mirroring the image, however, you need to take into consideration what exists outside of yourself, becoming aware that your first efforts serve as a model for your subsequent success. This "relationship to relationships" develops awareness of the consequences of your actions in your handwriting. When mirror images are done with a partner, the mirroring of forms then symbolizes the significance of one person's influence upon another. You might find this a stimulating source of conversation.

### MIRRORED CONNECTIONS

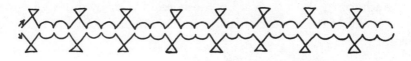

For your first mirror drawing you will practice the combined forms of Humps and Peaks, which mirror themselves as Cups and inverted Peaks.

Begin by making two Humps and then a Peak. Continue across the page, saying to yourself the name of each form as it is made. Follow this by making the reflected forms directly below the first line but not touching it, focusing only on form and space and using no verbal clues.

Do four lines of this mirrored drawing, and add it into your regular daily practice.

### TEEPEES AND HUMPS

Teepees and Humps further incorporate the two major connective forms of Garlands and Angles.

Begin at the baseline and make an upward diagonal line to the right. Then make a horizontal line across the top, followed by a downward diagonal that returns to the baseline. Make two rightward Humps and then repeat the first form. Continue across the page, keeping diagonals and horizontals at the proper angle and Humps rounded and even. Next, reflect this row of forms, leaving a slight space between image and reflection. Practice this exercise at regular intervals between the zonal form drawings.

*MIRROR FORMS*

Form drawings that mirror themselves can be drawn on a horizontal or vertical line. In her book *The Extra Lesson,* Audrey McAllen demonstrates some mirror drawings that are used in teaching children how to write. Though their creation is a shared effort between teacher and pupil, the same idea can be used by an adult working alone.

### *Mirror Forms*

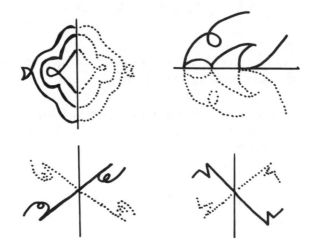

Draw a horizontal or vertical line and create your own design either on one side of the line or crossing it. Then make a mirror image of this form.

This exercise helps develop awareness of space and form, concave and convex features, and the directionality of each stroke. When folded in half, your mirror forms should approximate each other in size and shape. Try a few of these intermittently throughout your exercise sessions. The ability to reproduce lines in this way proves of vital importance in successfully copying letter forms.

## INTERPRETING YOUR RESULTS

Though the balance and control drawings are unlike actual letter forms, they help you develop mastery of line control and symbol reproduction.

The balance and control qualities developed in these exercises begin with the blank sheet of paper, which promotes higher awareness of the space handwriting will occupy, and the imaginary baseline upon which the handwriting rests. Think of your baseline as a tightrope, with each letter and letter group doing a balancing act upon it, like tightrope walkers or dancers. Are they gliding gracefully across the page, or are they teetering and tottering like amateurs?

Generally, a lack of horizontal flow in handwriting conveys qualities of weakness and ambivalence. Imbalance in visual form equates with a sense of psychological imbalance that could come across in your writing. A lack of baseline control will severely detract from the aesthetic quality of what might otherwise be highly legible handwriting. In the psychology of expressiveness, control in the handwriting suggests to the reader that a healthy, positive ego is at work and that an inner balance exists in the writer.

Whatever problems exist in your handwriting and whatever style of writing you are currently practicing, the balance and control exercises will be helpful, and even enjoyable.

*Garland Style writers.* Due to the rounded and sometimes soft effect of Garland Style writing, more-angled form drawings such as Wishbones, Stars, and the Maze are recommended. Wishbones are a highly stimulating exercise and can be practiced as a means of promoting sharp and consistent control in the script as well as rhythmic return to the baseline and a corresponding rhythmic cadence in the Middle and Upper Zones. The Stars and Maze exercises emphasize control of space and distance and are especially helpful for writers who like a bold, strong line formation.

*Arcade Style writers.* Mirror drawings should appeal to the artistic side of Arcade Style writers. Practicing these forms will bring you outside of yourself, making you aware of the results of your actions. Mirror drawings will be especially helpful to you if done with a partner, as illustrated in Audrey McAllen's book *The Extra Lesson.*

*Angle Style writers.* If you are an Angle Style writer, you may be tempted to increase pen grip and slow down writing movement due to the tense nature of your script. To avoid this, concentrate on keeping your index finger arched and using a medium writing pressure. Focus on the more rounded, relaxing forms such as the Clover, the Loop-the-Loop, and the Spiral.

*Thread Style writers.* If you are a Thread Style writer, you need to apply more definition of form and slow down your writing speed. The Maze and Stars will encourage you to do this, while Graduated Loops and the Loop-the-Loop will help you focus on making balanced forms in all three zones. Remember to always strive for a feeling of rhythm in the exercise movements, which will encourage consistent direction in your script.

*A final word of advice.* Balance and control exercises emphasize spatial awareness and are not necessarily geared to any one letter form. After the first two weeks of practice they can be done at any time, but they are especially helpful once you have mastered the zonal form drawings. Ideally, practice them first on a chalkboard and then on unlined paper.

Remember the principle of arrangement discussed in chapter 3: when doing a full page of forms, be sure to leave the same amount of space between each line and maintain balanced margins on each side of the paper. Do not allow writing lines or loops to touch or intertangle. The blank page represents your environment. Consider it a natural resource of writing space, to be used efficiently. Try all of the forms described in this book, but focus more on the ones that give you difficulty. For example, Angle Style writers may feel more comfortable with angular form drawings, but drawing these forms does not help the overall balance of their handwriting. Strive to recognize the benefits of each exercise regarding your own special style. Each exercise has something unique to offer.

Clovers, the Loop-the-Loop, and Graduated Loops are a subtle departure from the zonal form drawings. The Clover is a combined figure eight and Lazy Eight. It, like the Loop-the-Loop and Graduated Loops, should not be too difficult for you to make, though the upside-down Graduated Loops may take more practice. All three of these forms emphasize the natural flow of cursive handwriting.

Stars and the Maze emphasize control of space and distance, as do Spirals, which use a more rounded form. With the Maze and Spirals you are challenged to explore all the directions of space contained in movement. The rounded Spiral and the square Maze proceed right and then left, and their forms make you aware of an above-below, in-out movement, while a forward-and-backward motion is produced in their designs.

The mirror drawings help you achieve right-brain–left-brain balance and higher awareness of relationship in handwriting. Remember that a straight baseline along with balanced and rhythmic letter forms in your handwriting will project this personal, inner mastery.

Finally, if you find yourself doodling these forms long after your 30-day practice time, relax and enjoy it. Now, though, it is time to move on to actual letter-form exercises.

CHAPTER *9*

# Your New View
# of the Alphabet

*A*DAPTING THE FORM drawings to actual cursive letters is, of course, the final goal in your handwriting-improvement program. By diligently practicing the form drawings, you have accomplished the ultimate warm-up exercise that will lead you to developing a better handwriting.

**Purpose:** In this chapter you will see evidence for two kinds of legibility problems in handwriting: illegibilities *within* letters, and illegibilities *between* letters. The chapter will help you diagnose such problems in your script letter-by-letter and recommend corrective exercises.

**Method:** We will proceed through all the letters of the alphabet in the Middle Zone, Upper Zone, and Lower Zone, in that order. In each zone, we will look at problems with the letters and at problems in the connective strokes between them. By establishing which letter forms and connectives are causing illegibilities in your handwriting, you will focus your practice on those form drawings that will help alleviate these problems.

**Duration:** All exercise suggestions in this chapter are optional and are to be used at your discretion during the second half of the 30-day program and then afterward as needed. You need practice only those form drawings from chapter 7 and those letter forms that apply to your personal handwriting problems. The minimum effort would be to make one row of each applicable form, but the more you practice, the better your results will be.

**Terms to Remember:**

| | |
|---|---|
| Ballooning | Waistline connectors |
| Constriction | Beginning form |
| Closure | Following form |
| Retracing | Grounding |
| Baseline connectors | Release |

**Guiding Principles:** In this chapter you will blend the principles of movement, space, and form developed in the non-letter–form drawings with the simplicity, rhythm, and balance of each letter of the alphabet.

According to studies in the educational environment, 50 percent of all illegibilities are caused by four letters of the alphabet: *r, a, e,* and *t.* Illegibility often results from constriction in the loops of the *a* and *e* and inadequate or elaborated crossing of the *t.*

## HOW LEGIBLE IS YOUR HANDWRITING?

You may not have ever considered it, but in the lower-case letter forms in your handwriting, you actually have the opportunity to use two shapes for each letter: one when the letter begins the word, and one when it follows another letter. We call these the "beginning" and "following" forms. Basically, the difference is that the beginning letter form does not include a lead-in stroke, while the following form requires a connective stroke to join it to the previous letter. This chapter will help you see the components of each letter form in the same way an artist visualizes an image before committing it to canvas.

To establish which beginning and following forms and their connectives are causing illegibilities in your handwriting, write the following sentence. Write as you naturally do, without trying to form perfect letters.

The quick brown fox jumped over the lazily sleeping dog.

What is the value of this silly little sentence? It utilizes all the letters of the alphabet, with some in both beginning and following positions. By now you have probably seen the relationship between the form drawings of chapter 7 and the actual letter forms. Other unique combinations of those form drawings will be presented here to remedy specific letter-form and connection problems. To simplify the process, refer to the sample you just did to see which letter forms and connectives in your writing require additional practice.

## LEGIBILITY PROBLEMS OF THE MIDDLE ZONE

Most writing activity occurs in the Middle Zone, and where there is an abundance of script activity, there is likely to be confusion. Middle Zone letters include *a, c, e, i, m, n, o, r, s, u, v, w,* and *x.* We will list the legibility problems of each letter and then look at the illegibilities that occur in the connective strokes.

### The Letter *a*

Two common problems with the letter *a* result in a form that looks more like an *o* or a *ci* combination. This first problem relates to "grounding" and occurs when the final downstroke does not return completely to the baseline. The illegible *ci* combination is caused by incomplete closure.

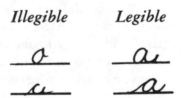

*Illegible*　　　*Legible*

If you find this problem in your handwriting, the following non-letter–form exercise sequence is recommended. Remember, these exercises allow you to concentrate on elements of movement, space, and form without the distracting requirement of rendering perfect letter shapes.

First practice a row of Ocean Waves.

Follow this with a row of Cups.

Combine these forms, alternating Ocean Waves and Cups.

After you have a satisfactory feeling for movement, space, and form in these exercises, join the elements of these forms into a row of the letter *a* that exhibits good closure and baseline grounding.

Your more legible result shows improved awareness of movement, space, and form and a higher degree of simplicity, rhythm, and balance of letter shapes.

### The Letter *c*

Legibility problems occur in the letter *c* when the top curl is not arched far enough to the right or when a loop occurs in the curl. Compression in the *c* form makes it point upward and causes it to be confused with the letter *i*; inadequate retracing of the return stroke results in a loop that can cause the letter to be mistaken for an *e*.

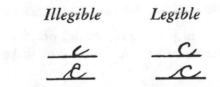

*Illegible*    *Legible*

If your script has a tendency to occasionally invite this confusion, try practicing Ocean Waves, alternating them with Little Loops and Cups as shown in chapter 7.

## The Letter e

Another common error in letter formation occurs when constriction in the writing of the letter *e* causes a retracing of the stroke, making the letter look like an *i*.

*Illegible*    *Legible*

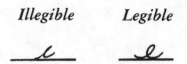

Reviewing the Loops and Cups combination exercise described in chapter 7 provides good practice for the movement of constriction and release.

There is an alternate form of the letter *e* that you may already use in your handwriting—the Greek *e*. This letter form can add a quality of style to your script when blended into it smoothly.

*Greek e*

## The Letter i

Lack of good retracing can result in a looping of the letter *i*, which then can be mistaken for an *e*. If the *i* dot is then forgotten or misplaced, confusion is unavoidable.

*Illegible*    *Legible*

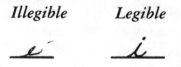

If this problem occurs in your handwriting, practice a row of Cups. Or, to make the exercise more interesting, first make a row of dots.

. . . . . . . . .

Then make a row of Cups beneath them.

### *The Letters m and n*

Concaved strokes in the letters *m* and *n* produce a false *w* and *u*, respectively, which can result in various legibility problems. Looped, concave humps on an *m* can cause the letter to be misconstrued as a *ue* combination. Looped, concave humps on an *n* can cause it to resemble an *ie* combination. In these poorly made forms the cadence of the letters has been inverted, causing the peaks to be made on top and the humps on the bottom.

|        *Illegible*        |        *Legible*        |
|:----:|:----:|

If this is a problem in your handwriting, begin your remedial practice with a row of Humps.

Follow this with a row of Peaks.

Now practice combining these forms by alternating the letters *m* and *n*.

The result will be a blending of Humps and Cups, with Peaks adding strength to the tops and retraced connections within the letters themselves.

### The Letter o

A common legibility problem occurs when the letter *o* is made like an *a*. This happens when the lead-in stroke from the *o* to the next letter fails to remain at the top of the Middle Zone. (In the correlation of zones with the physical body, this connective is known as a waistline connector.)

*Illegible*     *Legible*

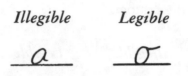

If this connective troubles you, you need to practice a row of Ocean Waves.

Follow this with a row of Castle Tops.

Now combine these forms, alternating Ocean Waves and Castle Tops.

Finally, combine an Ocean Wave and a Castle Top to form the letter *o,* making an Ocean Wave between each *o.*

A good drill would be to practice the letter *o* combined with every letter of the alphabet.

## The Letter r

The letter *r* can sometimes be mistaken for an undotted *i* when the second angle in the form is omitted.

*Illegible*      *Legible*

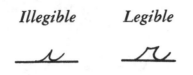

Practicing a row of Castle Tops is all that is required to make this letter more distinct. However, even the Castle Top *r* can sometimes appear like a Greek *e* when a ballooned loop appears.

*Illegible*      *Legible*

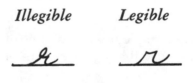

If there is an *r* problem in your writing, consider using the retraced version of the letter *r*, which connects easily to waistline-connector letters like *o* and *w*.

*Angled*      *Retraced*

## The Letter s

One of the most challenging lower-case letters is the letter *s*, which combines a Peak with an inverted Ocean Wave. The major legibility problem is generally a breakdown of form when the top of the letter shape is rounded and the bottom lacks closure.

*Illegible*      *Legible*

To strengthen the forming of the letter *s,* first practice a row of Peaks.

Now make another row of Peaks, but this time bring the second stroke to the left and retrace it back out to the right.

Think of this form not as letters but as a line of sailboats. This image may prompt you to make the proper closure on the bottom so your boats won't "sink."

### The Letter u

The letter *u* represents one of the simplest Middle Zone forms, and provides a good measure for the recommended standard distance between letters. Yet the *u* can sometimes be ballooned with a loop instead of the required up-and-down retracing that forms it, causing the *u* to be mistaken for either an *ei* or *ie* combination.

*Illegible*      *Legible*

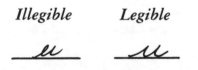

If *u* problems appear in your handwriting, practice the Cups exercise. Alternating Cups with other form drawings such as Little Loops, Castle Tops, and Ocean Waves can help you achieve the natural rhythm of cursive writing.

## The Letters *v* and *w*

The letters *v* and *w* are sometimes distorted into the letter *u* when their waistline connector is brought down to the baseline.

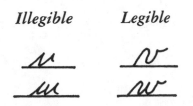

If you have difficulty with these two letter forms, the Cups and Castle Tops form drawings will help. Include a row of Peaks in your practice to add strength to these forms.

If your writing-style test was highly garlanded or arcaded, try to develop a more angled form of the letters *v* and *w*. Occasional angles can add strength to rounded handwriting.

## The Letter *x*

Though used infrequently, the letter *x* can sometimes cause legibility problems when its form is threaded out and improperly crossed.

To strengthen the forming of your *x*, first practice a row of Ripples.

Follow this with diagonals from right to left.

/ / / / / / / /

Then join these forms to make a row of *x*s.

*x x x x x x*

Practicing the Stars exercise described in chapter 8 will also help improve accurate placement of the final cross-stroke.

### Middle Zone Letters with Baseline Connectors

Whether a connective stroke is used with a particular letter depends on that letter's beginning position or following position in a word, and on your personal style. Middle Zone letters also incorporate the two basic types of connectors: baseline and waistline. When a letter's final stroke returns to the line of writing, it is said to have a baseline connector. The letters *a, c, e, i, m, n, r, s, u,* and *x* use baseline connectors.

Upper Zone

Middle Zone — Baseline

Lower Zone

The following examples demonstrate how Middle Zone letters with baseline connectors should be formed in their beginning and following forms. Because of its ease of movement, we will use the letter *e* as the "partner" letter.

| Beginning Form | Following Form |
|:---:|:---:|
| *ae* | *ea* |
| *ce* | *ec* |
| *ea* | *ae* |
| *ie* | *ei* |
| *me* | *em* |
| *ne* | *en* |
| *re* | *er* |
| *se* | *es* |
| *ue* | *eu* |
| *xe* | *ex* |

Notice that legibility improves in the beginning form when long lead-in strokes are omitted.

## Middle Zone Letters with Waistline Connectors

When a letter's final stroke does not return to the line of writing, it is said to have a waistline connector. The letters *o*, *v*, and *w* use waistline connectors.

| | |
|---|---|
| | Upper Zone |
| | Middle Zone |
| | Lower Zone |

Waistline

You may recall a childhood struggle in attempting to render these letters, especially their following form. The waistline ending stroke presents a challenge that may still inhibit your ability to form these letters. The following examples demonstrate the *o, v,* and *w* when they begin a word or follow another letter.

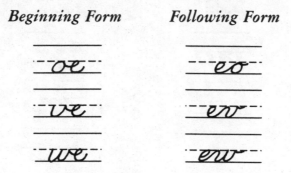

**Beginning Form**    **Following Form**

Some connectives have the straighter Castle Top form and some allow for a slight bending of the connective as seen in the Ocean Wave combination.

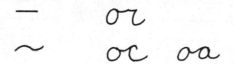

For rounded letters that follow *o, v,* or *w,* the connective may be made with a slight curve that helps to relax the stroke as it forms the adjoining letter.

## Exercising Your Middle Zone

Now that you know what is meant by Middle Zone letters and are aware that they contain two types of connective forms, you can practice these letters in combination. Using only the Middle Zone letters, make as many words as you can. Try to form words that incorporate the letters you have the most difficulty with and words that use these letters in both the beginning and following positions.

Some suggestions:

*arc*      *ox*
*car*      *ax*
*race*     *voice*
*erase*    *cave*

## LEGIBILITY PROBLEMS OF THE UPPER ZONE

The extended strokes of Upper Zone letters frequently result in legibility problems. Breakdown in form may make the *d, h,* and *b* appear like two letters instead of one. The unique quality of the *t,* which requires a necessary lifting of the pen to cross the stem, presents many opportunities for error.

### The Letter b

The waistline connector of the letter *b* creates a problem when it droops downward instead of staying above the baseline, causing the *b* to resemble an *li* combination.

*Illegible*      *Legible*

To correct this problem, practice a row of the Big Loop and Castle Top combination.

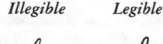

Next, add a Little Loop at the waistline of the letters. This practice will ease you into the proper connection of letters to this sometimes difficult waistline connective.

*bebebebe*

### The Letter d

A common confusion occurs with the letter *d* when a failure to join the Ocean Wave form with the *d* stem causes the letter form to resemble a *cl* combination. The *d* is one Upper Zone letter that is best written with a retraced upper loop.

| *Illegible* | *Legible* |
|:---:|:---:|
| *cl* | *d* |

If you need improvement on this letter, first practice a row of Ocean Waves.

Next, make sets of Swinging Bridges, but don't make the crossbars.

Now integrate these forms, emphasizing the proper closure. The secret is in making Ocean Waves that curl all the way to the right.

*ddd*

An alternate form of the *d* used by some writers is the delta *d,* which has a stylish look. However, its final upward stroke challenges natural cursive connections.

∂

*Delta d*

## The Letter f

See "Legibility Problems of the Lower Zone."

## The Letter h

Illegibility occurs when the letter *h* is made like an *li* combination due to a pulling away from the upper loop and a retracing of the hump.

**Illegible**          **Legible**

If you have a tendency to retrace the wrong part of this letter, try practicing a row of Big Loop–Little Loop combinations.

Next practice a row of Humps.

Combine these forms, making sure to retrace the downstroke of the Big Loop and the upstroke of the Hump.

With the retracing in the proper place, you now have a legible letter *h*.

## The Letter k

Legibility problems occur when the difficult letter *k* is made like an *h* due to improper indentation of the *k*-loop.

*Illegible*     *Legible*

If you have difficulty with this letter, try practicing a row of upside-down Little Loops.

Since speed is really the main problem with malformed *k*s, you should try doing a row of only this letter, concentrating on the indentation.

If you are still having difficulty, use a printed form of the *k* that can be made with one downstroke and then a quick in-and-out sideways *v*.

It is better to make a legible printed letter than an illegible written one. A few printed forms combined with cursive forms add to simplicity and even improve the picture value of your script.

## The Letter l

The letter *l*, when retraced or constricted, may appear as an uncrossed *t*. If the *l* lacks height, it may also appear as an undotted *i*.

Illegible      Legible

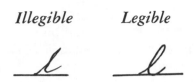

The best practice for this problem is to do a row of Big Loop–Little Loop combinations. If constriction appears throughout your writing, you would benefit from practicing both Propellers and Loop-the-Loop form drawings as a way of relaxing the tenseness in your script.

## The Letter t

The letter *t* presents many opportunities for misinterpretation. Though full loops are required for most Upper Zone letters, the *t* requires a retracing in the stem. The following are a number of illegibilities occurring with the *t* due to improper placement of the crossbar and elaboration and ballooning of the standard form.

Illegible      Legible

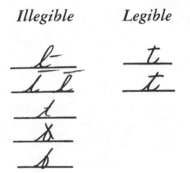

It's not hard to guess that the best exercise for the letter *t* is the Swinging Bridge. But more than this, the letter *t* requires strong horizontal and vertical pressure. A good way to achieve this is by practicing a row of Stars, described in chapter 8. Stars will help you place your *t*-crosses with precision and confidence.

## Upper Zone Letters with Baseline Connectors

Bearing in mind the concept of simplified beginning strokes, look at the following examples, which demonstrate how to shape the Upper

Zone letters with baseline connectors both when they begin a word and when they follow another letter. You will no doubt see how the earlier Middle Zone exercises facilitate your ability to shape most of the Upper Zone letters.

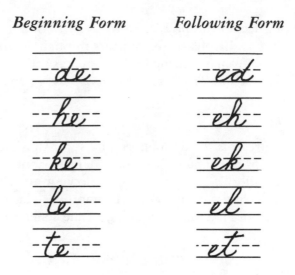

| *Beginning Form* | *Following Form* |
|:---:|:---:|
| de | ed |
| he | eh |
| ke | ek |
| te | el |
| te | et |

## Upper Zone Letters with Waistline Connectors

Only one letter of the Upper Zone group, the letter *b*, requires a waistline connector. The following illustrations show how the *b* is formed both at the beginning of a word and when it follows another letter. Several of its common consonant-cluster positions are also demonstrated.

| *Beginning Form* | *Following Form* |
|:---:|:---:|
| be | eb |
| bl | lb |
| br | rb |

Use the same curved form suggested earlier for connecting rounded letters to this waistline connector. You may also use either the angular *r* or retraced *r*.

### *Exercising Your Upper Zone*

Add the Middle Zone vowel letters (*a, e, i, o* and *u*) to the Upper Zone letters (*b, d, h, k, l,* and *t*) and see how many words you can make. Alternate their positions so that they appear in both beginning and following forms.

Some suggestions:

*bed             hall*
*bead         hallowed*
*bedecked   haunted*

## LEGIBILITY PROBLEMS OF THE LOWER ZONE

Creativity may compel you to overelaborate the Lower Zone of your handwriting, while fatigue will cause it to be de-emphasized. Speed also adds to legibility problems when Lower Zone letters appear at the ends of words. Fast writing tends to thread out, resulting in a breakdown of form and making it sometimes impossible to decipher. The Lower Zone letters *g, p, y,* and *z*, along with the trizonal letter *f,* can occasionally present such problems.

### *The Letter f*

The letter *f* can be confusing when made with a short and incomplete loop on either the top or bottom. The letter may appear as an *l* or an unfinished *q*.

*Illegible     Legible*

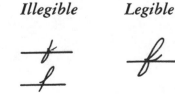

If your writing contains unrecognizable formations of this letter, practice a row of Big Loop–Little Loop combinations.

*elelelelel*

Follow this with a row of Pouches.

Join these forms to make the letter *f*.

If you prefer an alternate form, you can use a printed *f* that utilizes a waistline connector.

*f    fa*

This form works well at the beginning of a word but disrupts the flow of cursive writing if used in a following position.

### The Letter g

The letter *g,* when used at the end of a word, is sometimes threaded out, making it indistinct. This occurs often when it is used in the *-ing* ending.

| *Illegible* | *Legible* |
|:---:|:---:|
| *ing* | *ing* |

If the *g* gives you trouble, first practice a row of Ocean Waves.

Next practice a row of upside-down Little Loops and Big Loops.

Bring these two forms together to make a row of *g*'s.

A more fluid *g* form is the figure-eight *g.* This *g* has high style value and may be easier for you to make.

*Figure-eight g*

You should feel a natural flow when making this form. If you do not, it will only be an affectation in your script, causing your writing to look strained and artificial.

### The Letter *j*

When the dot of the lower-case *j* is misplaced or omitted, this letter form may be misinterpreted.

*Illegible*          *Legible*

As with the *i,* practicing a row of dots followed by Cups beneath them will help you be more precise in making this letter form.

### The Letter *p*

The letter *p* is prone to overelaboration or ballooning. Some writers have a tendency to add an upper loop on the *p* that is unnecessary and distracting. The *p* is also a letter that uses the inverted Ocean Wave.

*Illegible*     *Legible*

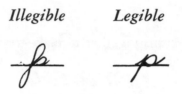

Practice of the Ocean Wave form will simplify this letter in your handwriting. The *p* is best written with a retraced lower extension rather than one that is looped.

### The Letter *q*

The letter *q* can be mistaken for a *g* when the descending loop is turned in the wrong direction.

*Illegible*     *Legible*

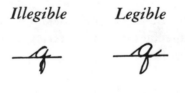

If you have difficulty with the *q,* practice its component forms—Ocean Waves and Pouches. First practice them separately; then join them to form the *q.* Follow these two forms with a Cup form and make a row of *qu* combinations.

## *The Letter y*

The letter *y*, like the letter *g*, can sometimes be threaded out at the end of a word. This occurs often in the *-ly* ending.

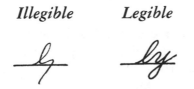

*Illegible*          *Legible*

To rectify this problem if it occurs in your handwriting, practice a row of Cups.

Then practice a row of Upside-Down Little Loops and Big Loops.

Bring these two forms together with regular Big Loops between each letter.

You may feel the same rhythm and movement that you experienced when practicing Propellers. A row of Propellers would also be beneficial for balancing both the Upper and Lower Zones of your writing.

## *The Letter z*

The letter *z* can prove illegible when made with an incomplete indentation. The infrequent use of this letter often results in a breakdown of its form.

*Illegible*  *Legible*

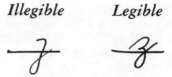

The *z*, like the letters *s* and *p*, has the inverted Ocean Wave in its form. A unique way to practice making the proper indentation for the *z* would be to make a row of Cups, but make the row vertical, starting at the top.

This form, paired with upside-down Big Loops, should help you improve your writing of the letter *z*.

### Lower Zone Letters with Baseline Connectors

Lower Zone letters require only baseline connectors, which are part of a general Garland configuration. However, the upward swing from below the baseline used with some of these letters may not always result in an easy Garland connection. The *g, j, y,* and *z* will usually swing into a more wavelike form to shape adjoining rounded letters, and into an upward-diagonal direction to connect with letters along the baseline.

*Beginning Form*    *Following Form*

*Beginning Form cont.*    *Following Form cont.*

Notice the difference in connection for the *g, j, y,* and *z* versus the *f, p,* and *q.*

## Exercising Your Lower Zone

Add the Middle Zone vowel letters (*a, e, i, o,* and *u*) to the Lower Zone letters (*g, j, p, q, y, z*) and the tri-zonal letter *f* and see how many words you can make while exploring connective relationships. Use letters in both beginning and following forms.

Some suggestions:

*jog          pig*

*joy          piggy*

*jogging      joyously*

Now that you have practiced the form drawings and letter forms for all three zones, incorporate them into words that use all three types of zonal letter forms.

Some suggestions:

*boy*      *beautiful*

*toy*      *handwriting*

*alloy*      *alphabet*

## THE SIMPLIFIED ALPHABET

Every workbook dealing with cursive handwriting presents a chart of idealized letter forms. The same holds true for this book, but something new has been added to the charts presented here. The beginning and following forms are shown separately, so that you may note the distinctive difference of the script when unnecessary beginning strokes are eliminated. Also, note the length of the ending stroke on each letter. None is too short or too long. You should bring the final stroke to the midpoint of the last letter, keeping it consistent with the spacing used between each letter.

### Lower Case—Beginning Form

*a b c d e f g h i j k l m*

*n o p q r s t u v w x y z*

### Lower Case—Following Form

*a b c d e f g h i j k l m*

*n o p q r s t u v w x y z*

## CAPITALS

Thus far our exercises have focused exclusively on lower-case forms for letters because they are the most frequently used. This book has a few simple suggestions for capital-letter forms.

Most of the capital-letter symbols modeled in existing copybook alphabets tend to elaborate on some element of their lower-case shape. We often apply extra curlicues, loops, and other embellishments, which make the letters more important and noticeable but harder on the eyes. It is recommended that you *print* capital letters rather than overelaborate their form. By adding a slight rightward slant and making the letters about two and a half times the Middle Zone height, your capitals will display enough size and shape to make them easily distinguishable from their lower-case counterparts.

### *Suggested Capital-Letter Forms*

$$A\ B\ C\ D\ E\ F\ G\ H\ I\ J\ K\ L\ M$$
$$N\ O\ P\ Q\ R\ S\ T\ U\ V\ W\ X\ Y\ Z$$

Most of these forms can be made without lifting the pen from the paper. Some retracing of downstrokes—for example, in the *B, M, N,* and *R*—and of the upstroke in the *U* make this possible. Again, strict adherence to form need not be the rule. As long as your writing remains legible, some alternate letter forms can be used. For example:

$$\mathcal{A}\ \mathcal{D}\ \mathcal{E}\ \mathcal{I}\ \mathcal{G}\ \mathcal{H}\ \mathcal{I}\ \mathcal{J}$$
$$\mathcal{M}\ \mathcal{N}\ \mathcal{P}\ \mathcal{Q}\ \mathcal{R}\ \mathcal{L}\ \mathcal{T}\ \mathcal{Y}\ \mathcal{Z}$$

Even with the alternate forms, however, unnecessary loops are best eliminated. Compare your capital letters with these and see if the simplified form complements your handwriting more than your current choice of letter form.

## CREATIVE CONNECTIONS

One other point in regard to either baseline or waistline connections is the use of unique connections between some letters. The *t*-cross, the *i*-dot, and the use of some printed letter forms such as the *f* allow for faster and more interesting connectives within your letter forms. You may use your ingenuity to decide if some of these connectives will work well in your handwriting.

Examples:

th fa in

In longer words you may even wish to use some intuitive breaks in your handwriting. This would be the case when writing extra-long words that may lead to fatigue or a breakdown of letter form. This lifting of the pen is similar to the airstrokes explained in chapter 3.

## NUMERALS

In the course of handwriting, we sometimes find it necessary to write numbers. In today's zip-code, checkbook, and credit-card society this is more true than ever before. Since numbers are used more often than not to convey money amounts, it is imperative that we make them clearly.

An efficient method for making numerals is to use one stroke whenever possible. The following forms are offered as possible models for your number formations.

0 1 2 2 3 4 4 5 6 7 8 8 9

## INTERPRETING YOUR RESULTS

It is understandable that your own preference for certain letters will be exhibited in your letter forms. Your main goal here is to improve your handwriting in order to make it more legible. Just remember that when your handwriting is illegible, you are defeating the main purpose of handwriting: to communicate clearly.

*Garland Style writers.* Garland Style writers frequently have more letter-form problems than connective problems, since Garlands are the natural connective form. Peaked forms added to your script will counterbalance the rounded connectives in your writing. The best places to incorporate these elements would be in the tops of the letters *m, n,* and *s.*

*Arcade Style writers.* Concentrating on simplicity in both the beginning and ending strokes of each word will help lessen the distraction of this style's umbrellalike elaborations. A few arcaded connections between words will appear rather artistic, whereas needless beginning and ending strokes will not.

*Angle Style writers.* Your script shows strength and determination—maybe even a little too much. Concentrate on keeping rounded forms round, avoiding the tendency to constrict and peak some loops, especially in the letters *a, o, p, l,* and *k.* Try for a Garland form in your connectives, and give them the approximate width of a copybook *u.*

*Thread Style writers.* Your main objective is making clearer letter forms. By utilizing some of the alternate letter forms, you may be able to achieve both speed and legibility in your handwriting.

No matter what your writing style, the diagnostic nature of this chapter will make you more aware of the problems in your writing and provide you with the means to overcome them. You are now equipped with the knowledge and skill that will make your handwriting a clear form of written communication. But there is one last aspect of your handwriting that we have not yet dealt with, one that involves a very important element of your public self-expression: your signature.

CHAPTER *10*

# The Bottom Line: Improving Your Signature

Now that you know how to make both the upper- and lower-case letters of the alphabet clearly, another important aspect of your handwriting can be addressed: your signature. The following insights, as well as a look at signatures of famous individuals, may help you project more expression in your signature.

**Purpose:** This chapter will offer you some insights into the importance of your signature and ways to enhance this very special form of self-expression.

**Method:** You will learn to integrate letter forms with other graphic expressions specifically related to signatures.

**Duration:** A short and simple handwriting demonstration will establish the best presentation for your signature.

**Terms to Remember:**
   Congruent signature

   Underscores

**Guiding Principles:** In the psychology of graphic expression, your handwriting represents your private self while your signature represents the public image you wish to project to the rest of the world.

## The Personal Meaning of Your Signature

When you entered the world as a newborn, no doubt great consideration was given to the name bestowed upon you. In school, your name became the first thing you were able to write. You may have formed the letters with a rather shaky ball-and-stick printed style, but the pride you felt in making and seeing your name on paper for the first time marked you as individual and special. Isn't it surprising, then, that this group of letters, which writers have made all their lives, is sometimes the most illegible part of their handwriting?

When you take a moment to ponder the number of times you have signed your name, you realize the staggering importance of your signature. When you sign checks, contracts, mortgages, and marriage licenses, your signature locks you into the full responsibilities of adult life. The signing of your name represents the most distinctive part of your handwriting and is probably the one group of letters you voluntarily practiced from the moment you learned their form.

Haste in writing frequently causes signatures to be scrawled. What message does that impart to the reader? A signature is the most public form of handwritten self-expression; it makes sense that it should be penned with clear and confident letter forms.

In Betty Edwards' book *Drawing on the Right Side of the Brain,* she presents various forms of a signature and states that "every time you write your name, you have expressed yourself through the use of line." Even from an artist's point of view, our signature and our handwriting have an expressive quality that transcends their daily communicative functions.

## Signature Congruence

Sometimes a writer's signature style is totally different from the style of the body of his or her handwriting. This gives the reader two different impressions of personality, and a sense that the writer is sending mixed signals. The degree to which the body of writing and the signature appear similar in form is called signature congruence.

*write and my signature is very similar.*

*Eldene Whiting*

*Body of writing with congruent signature*

*This is my normal handwriting*

*but my signature is much different*

*TRUCOUYNGUYEN*

Body of writing with incongruent signature

A congruent signature generally adds a quality of consistency to your signed, handwritten communications. But its importance really depends on whether it best supports the style you want to project to your reader. More than any other part of handwriting, a signature represents a written form of the ego and self-identity. By either simplifying or embellishing it, writers can choose how they will publicly display their degree of confidence and desire for recognition.

### Signature Consistency

Though unique, your signature is subject to the same amount of fluctuation as your everyday handwriting. Each time you sign your name the forms may vary slightly, yet the underlying consistencies remain.

Try doing the following exercise. Using four separate pieces of paper, write your name larger than usual on one page, then smaller than usual on another page. Sign with your right hand on the third sheet and then with your left hand on the fourth sheet. After completing your samples, find the midpoint of each signature by touching the beginning stroke of the first name to the ending stroke of the last name and folding the paper in half. You will discover that this midpoint bisects your signature at about the same point no matter how much fluctuation occurred in each signing. The spatial consistency evident in signatures provides one means of detecting forgeries.

## SYMBOLS IN SIGNATURES

Consistency in signatures extends beyond the graphic phenomenon demonstrated by your signature exercise. Consistency includes psychological expressiveness. In some signatures the signer uses symbols that are ego gratifying. The letter forms they choose reveal subconscious picture drawing, which projects some aspect of their public image. The symbol may be found in the actual letter forms, in beginning or ending strokes, or in the underscoring of the name.

*The signature of baseball player Roger E. Maris*

The signature of Roger Maris appears clear and normal to the average reader, but upon closer inspection you can find the tools of his trade—namely baseball. The upper stroke of his middle initial takes the form of a baseball bat; his *i*-dot resembles a fast-ball, and the *s* in Maris might be symbolic of the mitt he used in the outfield.

*The signature of Herbert Hoover*

In the signature of Herbert Hoover, who was President during the Depression, we find a symbol that emphasizes the troubling economic times of his administration. The letter *t* in *Herbert*, which joins with *Hoover*, has a very distinct dollar sign that testifies to his preoccupation with the financial state of the nation and with the world's devastated economy.

*The signature of entertainer Shari Lewis*

Some performers enjoy adding a special picture to their signature that projects their alter ego. The rounded, generous-looking signature of entertainer Shari Lewis is accompanied by a picture of her gentle and lovable "other half," Lamb Chop.

The outline of a ship in full sail with the crest of waves breaking on its bow can be seen in this sea captain's signature.

Double money bags appear in the lower zone of this mutual-fund treasurer's signature.

### A SIGNATURE EXPERIMENT

In the following exercise, sign your name as though you were in the following situations:

1. You have just pooled your life savings to buy the home of your dreams. Sign your name as if you were signing the bottom line of a mega–mortgage contract.

2. You are attending a night course to learn more about your favorite hobby. Sign the roll sheet to verify your attendance.

_____

3. You have received the gift you had hoped for from that special someone. Write a short note of thanks, and sign your name beneath it.

_____

4. Your rude neighbors have started a private junk heap in their backyard. When a petition is circulated to put an end to this eyesore, you can't wait to add your name to the list.

_____

5. You have taken on the duty of personally soliciting funds for your favorite cause. You give the form letters you're sending out a personal touch by signing your name at the bottom of each one. Sign the twenty-fifth letter of the one hundred you intend to send out.

_____

6. The last in a long series of office memos has made the rounds to your desk. You need to initial your acknowledgment and pass it along to the next employee.

_____

Does the test reveal different styles in your signature? Do they have different expressive qualities? Here's a basic description of the kinds of signatures you can use.

Samples 1 and 2 represent examples of a formal and informal signature, respectively. Obviously, the way you sign important documents may not be the same as the way you sign an attendance sheet. Your goal is to make sure that both these signatures project a positive image through their high form level and legibility.

Samples 3 and 4 indicate the influence of positive and negative emotional responses, respectively. With the note and signature of sample 3, you can observe the congruence of your signature with the words in your note. Is there a marked difference between the two, or are they basically the same in size and shape? If you have developed a more expressive signature than your normal script, you use the signing of your name as one more way of adding flair and showmanship to your ego display. If your signature is congruent with the body of your writing, you are more consistent and predictable, choosing to remain so even in your handwriting. In signature 4, you can observe the influence of anger in your handwriting. If your signature became more angled and heavier in pressure, you allow your emotions to interfere with your self-expression in handwriting. If you did not observe much change or difference in any of your signatures, perhaps you maintain consistent emotional responses regardless of the situation.

Sample 5 demonstrates the problem of fatigue in handwriting, especially in cases where people must sign their name repeatedly throughout the day. Recognize this as having a strong influence on the legibility of your handwriting, and use relaxation exercises and a more simplified signature to maintain some degree of consistency in the signing of your name.

Sample 6 is also influenced by haste and a nonchalant attitude. Quickly scrawled signatures may be convenient for the signer, but they can convey a feeling of detachment and can cause frustration in the person trying to read them.

So whether you are signing away your life, signing a roster, or simply initialing your acknowledgment, you need to develop a clear and legible presentation of your name. I recommend using your full name for important documents, keeping all letter forms discernible yet unique to your personal style. A combination of first initial and last name adequately serves for informal use, and a clear combination of your initials should be all that is necessary for quick approvals. Clarity of form will ensure that the signing of your name in any situation carries the power of firm endorsement that you intended.

# TYPES OF SIGNATURES

How often have you played with the formation of your signature? How many different ways do you sign your name, and under what circumstances do you change your signature style? If you stop and think about the times in your life when you felt the urge to change your signature, you will probably discover that some important decisions and events coincided with these times.

### The Squiggled Signature

I present this type of signature first because so many writers, especially businesspeople, enjoy telling me how they scrawl out their names. Their haste may be attributed to a heavy work load, the need to sign their name several times a day, or their general impatience no matter what the situation. A threaded signature could be interpreted as a signal that the writer does not have the time to communicate clearly and does not want others to find him out. The stiff, extended final stroke that sometimes completes these signatures suggests an untouchable quality and a preference to remain at a distance from others. Executive caution is the message—but remember, noncommunicative leaders can breed contempt among their subordinates.

### The Connected Signature

Connecting the capitals in the name is another way of expediting one's signature, as long as the letters remain readable. By not lifting the pen from the paper, writers can add speed to their signature while still maintaining some degree of legibility. The completed form projects the ingenuity and executive ability that went into this signature choice.

### The Circled Signature

Writers should always strive for some degree of simplicity in their handwriting, especially when writing their signature. Signers who like to add elaborations such as an arcaded stroke or a circle form around their name may be projecting an air of caution and self-protectiveness. This flamboyant elaboration creates a "magic circle of protection" around the name, which in handwriting represents the public ego of the writer. The reader may subconsciously feel that the signer is not an easily approachable person and perhaps is overly sensitive and elusive. The arcs and circles suggest a highly cautious nature and an inability to take responsibility for negative results. Covering a name may project a demand for privacy and imply a means of covering up mistakes to avoid blame.

### The Tangled Signature

An enmeshed signature that looks like a web or net defies identification. The scribbled lines of the tangled signature suggest that the writer does not want to be known or found out. The weblike formation of the name resembles a trap set to entangle and capture others. The graphic impression may be one of a writer who is wrapped up in himself, with little regard for others.

## UNDERSCORES

Underscoring a signature simply means that a writer chooses to draw a line under his or her name once the signing is complete. The rightward thrust of the line implies confidence and strong determination.

When the line takes a right-to-left direction, the writing movement is contrary to the normal flow and tends to emphasize the importance of the self over others. These writers' signatures appear self-centered and may imply to the reader a self-serving nature.

If in their haste some writers cross out their name rather than underline it, they could subconsciously be crossing themselves out. In essence, they are implying that they do not like themselves. This type of signature shows an effort to display confidence, but it misses the mark due to personal disappointment. The illegibility caused by the cross-out further distorts the image the writer wishes to project.

Variations in underscores send out many different messages. A wavy underscore expresses less strength and directness than does a straight line. The implied self-confidence of a straight underscore is modified, and a more flirtatious and fun-loving image emerges.

Two parallel lines added to either a straight or curved underline imply a concern for money and material possessions. The double lines symbolize those used to complete the dollar sign, and their use in an underscore subconsciously suggests a need for recognition based on status and financial success.

When the underscore becomes more elaborated than the signature, it may cause a visual distraction and create messiness in the writing.

Some writers' tendency to make a tornadolike drawing under their signature places emphasis and importance on their name as if they were elevated upon a pedestal. It implies to the reader that recognition and self-importance are of primary concern to the writer.

## INTERPRETING YOUR RESULTS

As with your normal handwriting, the number-one objective for your signature is that it be written legibly, using the principles of simplicity, rhythm, and balance. Choosing to add creativity to the capital letters is up to you, and is recommended as long as they can be read clearly. The lower-case forms should be made legibly, so that the entire name is readable. Any underscorings should be done in a left-to-right motion, avoiding any intertangling with the actual signature.

People in a hurry or those who have extremely long last names are prone to thread out their letters. Some shortcuts that still promote legibility can be the answer for them. If your full name is very long, you might consider using only your first initial and writing your last name more clearly. Connected initials or names may help you add speed to the signing of your name, but be sure that the letters of your John Hancock are distinguishable.

Extra strokes in a signature may or may not enhance its legibility. However, a clear, well-formed signature of high form level is less likely to be duplicated or misinterpreted. Don't be fooled by the common misconception that an illegible signature serves as a sign of your business acumen. Actually, illegible endorsements are truly inconsiderate. Last names can be spelled in many different ways. The time and patience it takes to interpret a scribbled signature will produce only irritation and frustration on the part of your reader. Ask yourself whether this is the impression you really want to make when signing on the bottom line.

*Garland Style writers.* Most likely Garland Style writers sign their names clearly and legibly. But the entire configuration of the signature may lack strength and confidence. If you are a Garland Style writer, you can add strength and confidence to your signature by using a straight and strong left-to-right underscore to complete your signature.

*Arcade Style writers.* Some of the most interesting signatures may be penned by Arcade Style writers. But, unlike writers of the other styles, Arcade writers will have a tendency to use encircled and elaborated additions when signing their names. Simplicity of form, with some Arcade connectives, will give a more legible and approachable appearance to your signature.

*Angle Style writers.* If you are an Angle Style writer, your signature may border on the illegible due to the many triangular and pointed strokes within it. A relaxing of forms is necessary. By using more rounded capitals and adding a firm underscore below your name, you can still project strength without having your signature appear too austere.

*Thread Style writers.* Thread Style writers are probably the number-one perpetrators of illegible signatures. If you are a Thread writer, consider this: your signature is *you.* Do you want it to be perceived as a squiggled line, or as the letter combinations that clearly state who you are? Developing simplified capitals and well-defined lower-case letters will help create a signature that warrants the recognition and acknowledgment you deserve.

You are now equipped with the knowledge necessary to better your handwriting from first line to bottom line. Keep in mind that the self-image you project through your signature is as important as any other form of self-expression.

CHAPTER *11*

## *Making the Change Permanent*

*T*HE CHANGES IN your handwriting are meant to last, but you may sometimes find yourself slipping into old habits. This chapter offers some suggestions to help you keep your script in top form.

What you have learned from the handwriting-improvement program presented in this book will provide you with the tools you will need to continue working on your handwriting for the rest of your life. You have practiced all the possible directions of writing movement, learned how to utilize space, and made the transition from form drawings to connected letter forms. Continued application of this integrated approach allows you to check and improve your preconscious handwriting habits.

From now on your focus will no longer be on just your writing hand and the pen you hold in it. You'll know these to be only the physical extensions of a complex eye-and-hand process coordinated by the brain. Handwriting really is brainwriting, but beyond that, it is a unique physical and mental expression of your optimal ability.

No matter how diligently you practice and perform the writing-movement exercises, your handwriting will always be just a little different from another person's. The research by Allport and Vernon mentioned in chapter 3 demonstrated that a highly educated theologian's handwriting appeared much different than a less-educated barber's script. If each of these men were to perform the writing exercises presented in this book, each would realize a clearer, more legible script. However, their individual form levels would still differ due to their aptitudes and the relationship of their vocations to handwriting.

Thus your aptitude and your need to write will affect the legibility and character of your script.

With this in mind, judge your handwriting based on your own ability and preference, and not by comparing it with anyone else's. Your handwriting, like your fingerprints, is a trait unique to you. This book offers you a variety of options for making conscious improvements in your personal script. This freedom of choice ensures that your handwriting will remain uniquely yours even as you effect change in it.

Initiating change in your handwriting is a continual process. Keeping the basic principles of this book in mind, you may become aware of other personal influences on your script. You may discover, for instance, that positive and negative events in your life will affect your handwriting. No matter what the cause, if you feel the desire to change something in your script, you now have the understanding, confidence, and skill to do this.

The pace your life-style requires must be a consideration when you are in the process of improving your handwriting. Simplified forms are best for the hectic times, while some elaborations may appear in your script when you have the time and are feeling fanciful.

Another area of script influence is your chosen occupation. Fields that require a great deal of printing or specific letter forms for graphs or schematics may encourage you to adapt this script as your personal style as well. Your own creativity will determine just how legible this adapted script becomes. A gentle blending of your occupational script with the forms suggested in this book will result in the best handwriting for you.

Whenever you are engaged in any of the exercises in this book— and for the rest of your life, for that matter—you are free from the ruler-wielding schoolmarm, overzealous parents, and the fateful, final judgment of the report card. You are in conscious control of effecting change in your handwriting through the free selection of exercises and optional letter forms and connectives that best suit the graphic image you wish to project.

The improvements you will see in your handwriting upon completion of the 30-day program are only the beginning of the changes you will witness. The more confident you become in your ability to master a new skill, the more this confidence will be reflected in your handwriting. After working through this book, you will have gained more than just an understanding of how to produce legible cursive handwriting. Your awareness of the personality projected in all handwriting and your practice of exercises that take you beyond mere letter form will give you a larger perspective that will continue to positively influence your writing style.

Remember, the goal of this program is to allow your expressive nature to come through in your script. Your letter forms need not be exactly like the copybook models. You may wish to continue your preference for larger or smaller letter forms, or for a more rightward or leftward slant. These features may manifest themselves in your writing as you see fit. Your appreciation of the expressive quality of handwriting lets you shape its forms to best represent you.

## Learned Models

The quality—or lack thereof—of your handwriting education, along with your sociocultural background, will have great influence on your attempts at improving your handwriting. If the level of difficulty you experience is high, it may evoke disappointment stemming from educational struggles in your past. Don't allow these old feelings to discourage you. Committed practice will result in a more creative awareness of movement and form, which in turn will improve the legibility and expressiveness of your cursive script.

While this book has encouraged you to simplify your letter forms for the sake of legibility, the elaborated forms of the typical American copybook alphabet with their extra loops and strokes may still appear in your script. That's okay. Remember, there is no right or wrong handwriting style. There is only what is natural for you and legible for your reader. No matter what letter-form variations appear in your daily script, try to make your letters as legible as possible, and avoid exaggerated size and unnecessary decorations.

There is a good chance that the cursive-handwriting instruction you were given in your youth was limited to proper pencil-grip and letter-form drills. If so, you were never introduced to the concepts of movement and space explored in this book. As a result, you probably never received classroom encouragement toward freedom of movement and simplified, fluid line style. So stay loose, and be creative. The act of handwriting should be enjoyable and relaxing, and the results should be a readable, personal expression you can admire.

### Keeping SCRIBE in Mind

The most important advice I can give you for improving your script legibility is to resist the urge to rush the act of handwriting. Keep it simple, but allow your own creativity to shine through. Pay attention to and try to control your inner balance and rhythm so that this same tempo can be reflected in your handwriting.

Every time you pick up a pen to write, say to yourself, "Simple, creative rhythm—inner, balanced energy." To help you remember this phrase, think of the acronym SCRIBE. In ancient times, a scribe was a highly trained specialist who served in an official, venerated position and who was considered influenced by the gods. The acronym will remind you of the free choice, conscious control, and personal style you now have the ability to project in your handwriting.

*Simple.* As in "Keep it simple." Simplicity in handwriting—one of the essential principles in this book—goes beyond just the elimination of unnecessary beginning strokes. There must be enough of the letter form present to make it recognizable to the majority of readers, and your goal is to find the right personal compromise between a totally skeletal letter form and an overelaborated or calligraphic one. Strokes should be efficient both in form and in the time it takes to shape them.

*Creative.* Freedom of choice is the creative element in your new approach to handwriting. You are not bound by any one letter form. Whether you are a Garland, Arcade, Angle, or Thread writer, you have the option to keep your style, and explore and improve its aesthetic qualities. Your understanding of the elements of arrangement help you utilize writing space in the same way an artist approaches a blank canvas. You want your final creation to evoke approval from others and self-satisfaction from within. You can also demonstrate your creativity by choosing efficient and unique connections between the letters in your writing. Baseline and waistline connectors are the directional guides, but as the fluency of your handwriting improves, you may find some ingenious ways to tie one letter to the next. The *t*-cross and *i*-dot offer interesting opportunities for creative connections. As you examine your spontaneous handwriting more closely, you may find some creative nuances you hadn't been aware of.

*Rhythm.* The rhythm of handwriting is found in the baseline cadence of strokes and in the upstroke and downstroke of each letter. The proper inhaling and exhaling learned in the Lazy Eights exercise brings energy into your handwriting and is reflected in these strokes. Color, shading, and the flow of the ink across the paper represent the lifeblood of the written word. Once this rhythm is evident in your handwriting, you will sense this same rhythm in all other aspects of your life.

*Inner.* *Inner* refers to the relaxation you can initiate within yourself through form drawing. This inner sense of calm can then be projected into your handwriting. Avoiding the tendency to rush the process of handwriting can be further enhanced when you realize that a steady and reliable inner guidance will prove more effective than frantic and scattered actions.

*Balanced.* By getting in touch with movement, space, and form, not only have you learned to improve your handwriting, you have touched on a spiritual balance within that has made you more aware of who you are and what you can become. The awareness of right- and left-brain influences also will help you utilize a whole-brain balance when practicing your handwriting. Balance further applies to the consistency of your form drawings, which is then transposed to your handwriting. As you realize how your writing mirrors your efforts, this balance becomes part of your entire self.

*Energy.* The energy you devote to your handwriting-improvement program will only increase your stamina and desire to continue these forms long after the 30 days are up. The projection of a healthy energy in your script will increase its form level and picture value and thus enhance the personality qualities you express in your writing.

The following chart lists all the exercises included in your four-week handwriting-improvement program. A suggested schedule of exercises is offered, but keep in mind that every writer's needs and abilities will vary.

## Handwriting Exercise Chart

| Activity | Week 1 | Week 2 | Week 3 | Week 4 |
|---|---|---|---|---|
| *Warm-up Exercises* | | | | |
| Two Wheels | X | X | X | X |
| Lazy Eight | X | X | X | X |
| *Right/Left-Brain Exercises* | | | | |
| Fountains | X | X | O | O |
| Triangles | X | X | O | O |
| Diamonds | X | X | O | O |
| Downstrokes | X | X | O | O |
| Cross-Strokes | X | X | O | O |
| Fantasy Animals | X | X | O | O |
| *Finger Exercises* | | | | |
| Tabletop Gymnastics | X | O | O | O |
| Blind Man's Bluff | X | O | O | O |
| Climbing the Ladder | X | O | O | O |
| The Cross-Over | X | O | O | O |
| *Middle Zone Form Drawings* | | | | |
| Little Loops | X | X | O | O |
| Cups | X | X | O | O |
| Humps | X | X | O | O |
| Peaks | X | X | O | O |
| Ocean Waves | X | X | O | O |
| Castle Tops | X | X | O | O |
| Ripples | — | X | O | O |
| Loops and Cups | — | X | O | O |
| Humps and Cups | — | X | O | O |
| Cups and Castle Tops | — | X | O | O |
| Double Waves | — | X | O | O |
| *Upper Zone Form Drawings* | | | | |
| Little Loops and Big Loops | — | — | X | O |
| Big Loops and Castle Tops | — | — | X | O |
| Swinging Bridge | — | — | X | O |
| Propellers | — | — | X | O |
| *Lower Zone Form Drawings* | | | | |
| Upside-Down Little Loops and Big Loops | — | — | X | O |
| Propellers | — | — | X | O |
| Pouches | — | — | X | O |
| *Balance and Control Exercises* | | | | |
| Clovers | — | — | X | X |
| Loop-the-Loop | — | — | X | X |
| Graduated Loops | — | — | X | X |
| Wishbones | — | — | X | X |
| Stars | — | — | X | X |

## Handwriting Exercise Chart (continued)

| Activity | Week 1 | Week 2 | Week 3 | Week 4 |
|---|---|---|---|---|
| The Maze | — | — | X | X |
| Spirals | — | — | X | X |
| *Mirror Drawings* | | | | |
| Mirrored Connections | — | — | X | X |
| Teepees and Humps | — | — | X | X |
| Mirror Forms | — | — | X | X |
| *Letter Exercises* | | | | |
| Middle Zone Letters | — | X | O | O |
| Upper Zone Letters | — | — | X | O |
| Lower Zone Letters | — | — | X | O |
| All Letter Forms | — | — | — | X |

The chart recommends a gradual introduction of each exercise, building toward greater mastery as you progress. Remember, each writer has different needs and a different momentum for learning. Some of my students have mastered the program in just three meetings, while others require remedial work on a continuing basis.

## Finding Your Special Pen

We may happily use most any pen close at hand to write with, but most writers have some idea of the instrument that works best for them. Is there a particular pen you hate to use? Is there a favorite in your desk? Have you ever wondered what the difference is between these pens?

You've learned a new skill. Why not make it even more enjoyable by selecting a quality writing instrument to accompany your improved handwriting? There are a number of fine writing instruments on the market. The type of line your pen produces, whether you've chosen a low-cost ball-point or a gold-nibbed fountain pen, will have an influence on your handwriting personality.

The pride of pen ownership may be just what it takes to help you maintain permanent change in your handwriting. If you make a special effort to obtain a pen that has character, style, and personal value, it can serve as an incentive to produce writing that shows these same qualities.

Statistics show that most owners of finer-quality pens are in responsible, influential positions. A top-of-the-line pen may serve as a talisman, a sacred object that brings good luck and represents the prowess of its owner. And you can impress your reader with both your writing form and the stylish way you choose to leave your mark.

Art and technology have continued to influence the development of the pen point and the ink it distributes. In better-made ball-points the ball is covered with microscopic etchings that allow a more even flow of ink. And the viscous properties of the ink reduce the possibility of smearing.

Roller-ball pens afford the ease of movement attributed to ball-point pens, but the lines they produce resemble those of a fountain pen. Like ball-points, roller-balls have ink-cartridge refills in appropriate writing colors. The utilitarian nature of both ball-points and roller-balls makes them reliable everyday instruments for note taking and for use with carbon forms.

Felt-tip pens mimic the design of the reed pens of Egypt. The thicker ink line of the felt-tip may project a false sense of self-confidence in the handwriting because less pressure is required. The easy movement and varied colors of these pens make them good practice pens for children just beginning their form-drawing exercises.

Fountain pens truly invite elegance in their design. The nibs of these pens can be of 14- or 18-karat gold or a gold-and-platinum alloy. Modern fountain-pen inks are designed to be nonclogging and distinctive in color. Filling a fountain pen does not require the old lever-and-pump action of earlier models. Today's quality instruments are filled by using either a cartridge or a piston-action mechanism. Cartridges need merely be inserted into the pen barrel, while the piston action requires a dipping of the pen nib into an ink bottle. A quick twist on the top of the pen, and it fills automatically.

I know I have a different sense about my handwriting depending on which pen I use. An analysis of all the elements of your handwriting, including your choice of pen, can only help you further assess the material, procedure, and form that are best for you. In any case, choose a pen you are comfortable with, and one that will not be offensive to the reader's eye due to an odd color of ink or inconsistent flow.

## A Relaxation Process

You may discover that the writing exercises in this book will help you to relax, organize your thoughts, and focus your energies. They provide both a mental and a physical workout. I use the term *workout* because the exercises can be physically stimulating and invigorating. Working in the ideal format of a large chalkboard or butcher paper, and working to the beat of music, the right-brain–left-brain exercises, warm-up exercises, and finger exercises all take you beyond the familiar seated position of most learning environments.

While doing the handwriting-improvement program, try to incorporate physical exercise into your life as much as possible. Aerobics, brisk walks, gymnastics, and even playing the piano all contribute to balance and whole-brain thinking. The healthy feeling you develop from proper exercise will enhance your coordination, and, no doubt, will shine through in your handwriting.

For a change of pace, try doing the exercises somewhere other than in your usual work area. On the job, you can purchase a large desk-pad calendar and doodle your favorite forms as you conduct your telephone business. At home, by leaving some writing paper and pens near each telephone you can both take messages and practice your form drawings as you carry on your conversations. If you are a cronic doodler, you can transform this idle pastime into useful practice.

Here's one more suggestion, but one you are certain to avoid, as have all generations before you: try writing more letters. You have learned a new art form; now put it to use by doing some of your correspondence in longhand. Quick thank-you notes are good business practice, and handwritten family letters will convey an intimate quality that will make your effort seem extra-special.

## Change Your Handwriting, Change Your Personality?

The motivation to improve your handwriting may even go beyond the obvious need for legibility. Allport and Vernon presented evidence that handwriting is a form of self-expression, and graphologists contend that handwriting is a map of your personality. So if the writing changes, will the writer follow suit?

A branch of graphology known as graphotherapy claims this to be true. Of course, as is the case with "the chicken and the egg," it may be difficult to tell which happens first: a change in the writing, or one in the writer. If your writing changes when *you* change, then why not speed up the process by changing your writing to change you? This belief is the basic tenet of graphotherapy—that behavioral corrections can be initiated by correcting the corresponding factors in the handwriting.

For example, if a writer tends to procrastinate, this behavior may be evident in the weak *t*-crosses in his handwriting. A graphotherapist may prescribe that he or she write an affirmation such as "I complete my tasks in a timely and efficient manner," with instructions to place strong and firm *t*-crosses about three-fourths of the way up the stem. In doing this the writer is subconsciously telling himself or herself to be more dutiful and efficient.

I do not profess to be a graphotherapist, but I do believe that if you really feel that changing your handwriting will help you feel more confident and accomplished, it really doesn't matter what you call the process. Both graphotherapists and handwriting therapists are dedicated to helping you make changes. If change in your writing is accompanied by internal change too, so much the better.

## *Mental, Physical, and Psychological Benefits*

Finally, the handwriting exercises presented here are holistic. Not only will your handwriting improve, but you may experience feelings of improvement in all that you do. The artistic quality of each form drawing may be the catalyst that awakens your talents in drawing, painting, sculpting, and other artful forms of self-expression. Your awareness of movement may add to your grace in walking, dancing, and other physical activities. Your understanding of the proper utilization of space may trigger clearer thinking and an appreciation for decor. And your new awareness of form can be further nurtured in areas such as photography and design.

Whatever your interest, you will find the principles presented in this book helpful in more than just improved handwriting. You will discover an improved *you!*

Best wishes, and happy handwriting!

# A Note to Parents and Teachers of School-Age Children

$T$HOUGH THIS BOOK is written primarily for adults interested in improving their existing handwriting, the main features of the exercise program were established with the child in mind. The scribblings and games are the perfect medium for introducing the techniques of cursive handwriting to the unfamiliar hand.

Young children naturally feel joy about learning their letters and graduating into cursive forms. But this joy can turn to frustration when somewhere along the line they encounter a learning roadblock, or are deprived of supportive, progressive instruction, or both.

Handwriting instruction in our schools has diminished significantly in recent years. However, there is the hope of renewed interest in penmanship as important subject matter. I believe a creative instructional approach such as the program outlined in this book, adaptable to any copybook style for home or institutional use, is essential for this revival to take hold.

Letter forms by themselves project a highly complex form to the young learner. What a child perceives in the letter form is not always what was intended in conventional instruction. Presenting the child with the entire alphabet all at once, with its upper- and lower-case forms and its many directional changes, frequently results in misperceived visual information. This problem can be compounded when children are converting from ball-and-stick forms to cursive script. The child's ability to retain the memory of each stroke sometimes leads to confusion of forms. For example, one student of mine began to incorporate the beginning circle of the capital $M$ into the formation of his lower-case *m,* and he adamantly argued with me that this was the way his teacher told him to do it.

*The model*          *The perception*

In a program based on skill development through preliminary non-letter–form exercises, simplicity of movement and form eliminates the possibility of misinterpretation. As each successive form is mastered, the student can be helped to see how certain forms or a combination of forms contribute to the formation of each letter. It is during the crucial time before the child even begins to make letters that any perceptual confusions can be corrected. Misunderstandings can be cleared up through noncritical, nonjudgmental discussion of form. Young learners need not experience the disappointment of seeing red marks on their penmanship papers or the potential negative attitude patterns that can develop.

Based on my experience, I suggest that parents and teachers who wish to use this book in working with children keep it light and keep it fun. Avoid comparisons with siblings or schoolmates. The learning-handicapped children I work with often have a brother or sister who not only adapts well to traditional educational methods, but also excels in academic achievements. Living in this shadow only blocks the child more and leads to emotional problems that will surely appear in the handwriting. Also, remember that physical and psychological problems generally manifest themselves in the handwriting. For instance, if children are tired, their handwriting frequently slants downhill. If you stand over them, forcing them to practice the exercises, their writing will be tense and full of angles.

In developing a child's interest, start out with Little Loops, and then introduce the spatial awareness game known as Pyramid. To play Pyramid, you make a loop that will establish the pinnacle of the design. The child then adds a two-loop line below, with the instruction to keep the size and spacing consistent with the first loop. Each writer takes turns until the width of the paper allows for no further "pyramid building."

Help the child with even, well-spaced loop placement from line to line as you proceed to the base of your structure. If there is a loop above one writing line, a space should appear below it. You can correct any spatial-arrangement problems the child has when you make your alternating lines. In this way, the concepts of movement, space, and form subtly present themselves to the child.

To make this exercise even more enjoyable, you and the child can take turns crossing out as many connected loops as you desire. The object of the game is to leave one last loop for the other player. Cross-outs can be made only horizontally. Once a line has been drawn through a loop, no other lines may pass through it. Keep the pace of the game quick, to minimize any mathematical strategy and to promote vigorous movement and pen pressure.

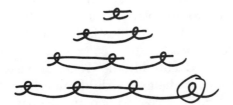

Another game children enjoy is Soccer. Two players are required, which makes this an excellent game for the tutorial environment. Using a chalkboard (mine was usually laid on top of the writing table), mark four positions using the letters *a* through *d*, and draw a "goal net" at one end.

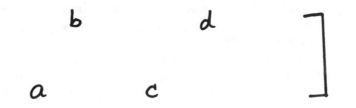

Teacher and student take turns being "kicker" and "goalie." To kick, the writer must first "squiggle" his or her way from *a* to *b* to *c* to *d,* making connected circular movements, and then try to shoot into the "net." In order to distract the goalie, the kicker may go back and forth among the letters as many times as he or she likes, as long as the movement conforms to alphabetical order—for example, from *a* to *b* to *c* to *b* to *c* to *d.* At the same time, the "goalie" writer uses the same squiggling movement within the goal area to try to "block the kick." After a game, the board should look something like this:

I usually use Soccer with my less aggressive students since I like to keep all of my fingers in working order. The continual motion helps reinforce the connectedness required in cursive writing and also promotes rounded forms. Sometimes after practicing form drawings, my students ask, "Can we just play soccer for a while?" What they perceive as a break is really a continuation of practice, but with a little fun added for good measure.

I recommend introducing Middle Zone form exercises first, a few at a time. Do not overwhelm the child, especially if he or she finds the forms too difficult to make. When an adequate number of forms have been mastered, have the child practice words composed only of the Middle Zone letters. For example: mastery of Little Loops, Humps, and Cups, along with Ocean Waves, enables you to introduce the letters *a, c, e, i, m, n, o, u, v,* and *w.* The children may even try to make silly sentences that incorporate their words.

After the Upper Zone and Lower Zone form exercises are introduced, follow the same procedure, blending in the Middle Zone forms. Quickly and effortlessly all the letters of the alphabet will be introduced and assimilated with a firm understanding of their movement, space, and form relationship.

Follow the steps listed in chapter 5, using as much sensory-awareness technique as possible—writing in the air, on the tabletop, with chalk, and with pencil. Musical accompaniment adds yet another dimension to the learning environment. Such a multisensory approach will correlate with some aspect of each child's individual learning style.

No matter what technique you use, you will encounter at least one student who simply cannot physically respond to the exercises. Let this be your first clue to major learning difficulties. Such a child must be examined by a physician familiar with learning problems, and the school must be notified of the diagnosis. With this information, the school system is obliged by law to meet the special needs of the different learner. When I began teaching my handwriting-improvement program, I never intended to become an advocate for young students considered learning disabled. But my experience with many children of widely varied skill levels has provided me with convincing, firsthand evidence of the relationship between handwriting and a learner's physical, psychological, and physiological problems.

An eleven-year-old student of mine, Ryan M., is a perfect case in point regarding the special care that learning-different students need and deserve. Ryan was brought to me by his mother, who wanted him to improve his handwriting and felt that he needed more personal attention than his special tutor could give him. He was enrolled in a public school, had participated in adaptive PE classes, and had attended a learning-handicapped class for special tutoring in math. Physically, he was of slight build and appeared healthy.

His mother and I set up an initial six-week program of one hour a week. Ryan was cooperative, but his attention span lasted, at most, a half hour. At our sessions, he always wore his baseball cap and kept his eyes averted downward. Though he could be playful, he was never difficult to manage.

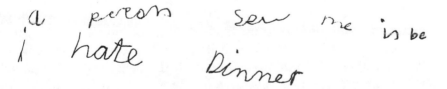

*Ryan's handwriting before therapy*

Ryan's initial handwriting sample displayed an extreme lack of consistency and control. He had difficulty in forming the letters, with errors made in both form and direction. His writing had no definite margins or spacing, and he tended to write off the edge of the paper.

My first attempts at improving his handwriting failed. Then, when I observed him writing on the chalkboard even though his piece of chalk had worn down, I realized his situation required closer examination. It was obvious that Ryan had finger agnosia, but he was also unable to walk a chalk outline of a form drawing I had made on the ground. His problems were being caused by something more than a lack of feeling in his fingers. I asked his mother to take him to the doctor for an intensive physical examination.

At last we discovered a medically based reason for his problems: the pediatrician diagnosed Ryan's condition as developmental Gerstmann syndrome. This condition creates problems with direction, with distinguishing right from left, and with understanding one's place in time. Its symptoms also include dysgraphia, which explained Ryan's problem with writing, and dyscalculia, which causes problems with math and sequencing.

Ryan was able to improve through special handwriting exercises. I developed a legible signature for him and created a printscript for him to use when he absolutely had to write down information. I created an entire workbook for Ryan, entitled *The Ryan Alphabet.* When I presented it to him, he beamed with delight at having something named after him. Then he asked, "But, what are you going to do for other kids whose name isn't Ryan?" I told him that it would always be called *The Ryan Alphabet* in honor of him. The smile I got in return was worth all the hard work that had gone into tutoring him.

*The Ryan Alphabet,* of course, had to present a simple alphabet and in some way circumvent Ryan's problem with directional confusion. I certainly could not offer instructions such as "Draw a loop to the left" or "Draw a loop to the right" or refer to up-and-down movement. My solution was to use a lined page, placing a vertical green line on the left and a similar red line on the right. The two colored lines signified the beginning and end of the page, respectively, with the traditional meanings of green for "go" and red for "stop." This satisfied Ryan's horizontal-movement problem, but vertical movements were also necessary to form letters. Positive results occurred when I placed a sun at the top of the page and moon at the bottom. The symbolism of rising and setting helped Ryan develop a sense of directional flow from the top of the paper to the bottom.

For the actual printscript forms, only two specific shapes were presented, a horseshoe and a straight line. A sample of these exercises follows.

Horseshoes: from red (right) to green (left) and end toward red:

From green (left) to red (right) and end toward green:

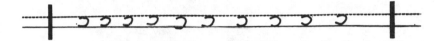

Up from green, down on red side:

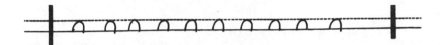

Down from green, up on red side:

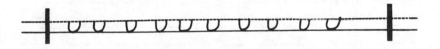

Straight lines: start up at sun and go down to moon, through dotted line, stop at second solid line:

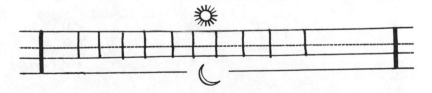

Start at broken line and go down from sun to moon, stop at first solid line:

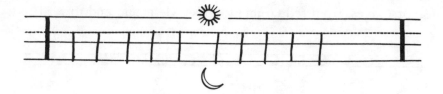

Start at broken line and go down from sun to moon, stop at second solid line:

Ryan's printscript letters are drawn as follows. All letters are made in a single movement whenever possible. With the addition of only a few diagonal lines, most letters can be made by using some form or combination of horseshoes and straight lines.

*Ryan's printscript*

I went to today and I have a School lot of homework.

*Ryan's handwriting after therapy*

Because of his hectic school schedule and the extra time his mother devoted to helping him with his work, Ryan received my tutoring for only the agreed-upon six weeks. His final sample still shows some directional problems in spacing and the misplacement of words due to corrections, but the letters are much clearer and more well defined.

This case has a happy ending. Because Ryan has a medically diagnosed learning disability, the school allows him to use a computer for written assignments and must provide him with tapes of his lessons so that he can listen along as he reads his assignments.

In working with any child, it is imperative that teachers and parents be aware of possible learning blocks that may manifest themselves in the child's handwriting. Think of handwriting as one more measuring tool in assessing a child's personal learning style.

# Glossary

**Agnosia.** See *Finger agnosia.*

**Angle.** One of the four basic connective forms in handwriting. Angles force an abrupt change of direction, which breaks the flow of the writing movement. Angles may be found within letters or where one letter connects to another.

**Aphasia.** Loss of the power to speak or to understand speech, depending upon whether the trauma occurs in the motor or sensory area of the brain. Developmental aphasia is a condition that exists from birth. Acquired aphasia is caused by trauma from injury or surgery.

**Apraxia, developmental.** A failure in development of normal skills, causing abnormal clumsiness that affects learning and coordination.

**Arcade.** One of the four basic connective forms in handwriting. An arched stroke resembling an architectural arcade, closed at the top and open at the bottom. A reversed Garland.

**Arrangement.** The manner of distribution and organization of the writing on the page. The total pattern of margins, word space, zonal proportion, and slant.

**Balance of writing.** Writing is balanced when the slant, pressure, and letter forms are consistent.

**Balance of zones.** Balance of zones occurs when the Upper Zone and Lower Zone extensions are similar, giving a balanced look to the writing. The recommended dimensions are a Middle Zone of three millimeters and Upper and Lower Zones of two millimeters above and below the Middle Zone, respectively.

**Ballooning.** See *Fullness.*

**Baseline.** The line, real or imagined, established by the writer, upon which the letters rest. It may be even, uneven, erratic, or sloped.

**Beginning stroke.** An initial stroke. The beginning of a letter or word, not necessary to the basic letter form. It may be a short or a long stroke. It may be a flourish, a straight stroke, or a curved stroke.

**Bizonal.** A writing movement that encompasses two zones. The Upper Zone letters (*b, d, h, k, l, t*) and the Lower Zone letters (*g, j, p, q, y, z*) are bizonal.

**Book of Kells.** A work written using the Irish half-uncial script, which, though influenced by the Roman script, was expanded to include its own form of majuscule and minuscule alphabets.

**Brainwriting.** A term coined by Wilhelm Preyer, a medical doctor interested in handwriting analysis. The expressive writing movement peculiar to each individual.

**Cadence.** The rhythmical pattern of the writing stroke as it returns to the baseline; especially noticeable in the letters *m* and *n.*

**Calligraphy.** A method of script writing in which specially designed pen nibs are used to create beautiful writing.

**Capital letters.** Enlarged letters, often embellished, used at the beginning of a sentence or proper name.

**Clarity.** A quality of writing that is distinct and legible. Letters are open and clearly formed, and strokes are clean-cut and easy to read.

**Connective form.** The distinctive form of writing structure that connects letters and parts of letters. The most common are Garlands, Angles, Arcades, and Thread.

**Consistency.** Regularity in the handwriting. The repeated pattern or use of individual letter forms. This may take the form of monotonous repetition in low-form-level writing or a rhythmic consistency in high-form-level writing.

**Contraction/release.** See *Tension/release.*

**Copybook.** The normal standard form of writing used in schools as a model for students to imitate. Each language has its own copybook standard.

**Corpus callosum.** The large bundle of nerve fibers connecting the right and left cerebral hemispheres.

**Cross-dominance.** A condition where there is a lack of sidedness based on brain dominance. A mixture of right and left dominance based on eye, hand, and foot preference.

**Cuneiform.** A system of writing developed by the Sumerians around 3500 B.C. Its wedge-shaped forms began the transformation of simple pictures into a systematic written language.

**Cursive writing.** Continuous writing in which letters are connected within words as prescribed by a copybook model.

**D'Nealian®.** A style of writing that teaches a print script that can be easily transformed into cursive writing.

**Doodles.** Scribbling. Pencil play while one's mind is otherwise occupied. The record of the unconscious brain as an illustrated form. Mechanical, half-conscious releases of surplus mental energy. Doodles take many forms: dots, loops, geometric shapes, or single lines that arrange themselves into chance agglomerations or well-organized wholes.

**Downstroke.** A stroke made with a downward motion of the pen as a partial or complete part of a letter or diacritic.

**Dyscalculia.** A learning disability that causes problems with numerical manipulation.

**Dysgraphia.** A learning disability that directly affects the ability to write. The inability to execute motor movements required to write or copy written letters or forms. Or the inability to transfer the input of visual information to the output of fine motor movement. Or various combinations of both these conditions.

**Dyslexia.** A learning disability resulting in a faulty processing of printed information in the left hemisphere (the verbal lobe), which causes reading and writing problems.

**Dyspraxia.** See *Apraxia, developmental.*

**Elaboration.** Any addition to the copybook standard of handwriting that is not needed as a part of the basic letter form.

**Ending stroke.** The final stroke or flourish of a letter or word after completion of the full letter form.

**Expressive movements.** Graphic patterns recorded in the movement of handwriting that reflect the dynamic processes within the personality.

**Final.** See *Ending stroke.*

**Finger agnosia.** A condition that causes a loss of the power to recognize the import of sensation in the fingers.

**Flourish.** A decorative stroke used as an accessory to the standard letter form.

**Form.** The shape of letters, punctuation, and any other writing element that creates a style of writing unique to the individual.

**Form drawing.** A process by which designs are practiced to reinforce and enhance the learning of handwriting based on movement, space, and form.

**Form level.** The quality of writing judged by its overall appearance. It usually involves organization, shading, simplicity, rhythm, originality, and dynamic forward movement. Handwriting may be judged to be of either high or low form level.

**Fullness.** Writing that encompasses more of the writing surface than is prescribed by school standards, sometimes referred to as ballooning of loops. Usually found in the Upper and Lower Zone loops, but also may be found in Middle Zone formations, especially in oval letters.

**Garland.** One of the four basic connective forms in handwriting. Shaped like a cup, the Garland connects the downstroke of a letter to the following upstroke with an open curve. It is the simplest of left-to-right movements in writing.

**Gerstmann syndrome, developmental.** A learning disability that creates problems in appreciating one's position in space; the inability to order or sequence objects or ideas around oneself; the inability to make relative sense out of environmental demands.

**Graphologist.** One who analyzes handwriting as a means of determining personality traits and vocational skills.

**Graphology.** A method of determining the character and/or personality of a writer through a study of his or her script. Derived from the Greek *grapho,* meaning "I write," and *logos,* meaning "language," "word," or "statement." Coined by Abbé Hippolyte Michon in 1872.

**Graphotherapy.** A counseling technique that attempts, by changing handwriting style, to induce beneficial changes in the writer's attitude and/or behavior.

**Greco-Roman alphabet.** Our modern alphabet consisting of twenty-six letters in both upper and lower case; influenced by the early Greek and Roman alphabets.

**Half-uncial script.** A writing form developed by the Irish and recorded in the Book of Kells. Its forms include both captial and lower-case alphabets.

**Handedness.** The preferred use of one hand over the other. The dominant hand is superior in its motor aptitude, quickness, muscular strength, manual skill, and tactile discrimination. The majority of writers are right-handed, with approximately 10 percent of the population preferring the left hand.

**Handwriting.** The graphic equivalent of speech. A system of letters, words, and symbols used to communicate thoughts, ideas, or messages.

**Handwriting analysis.** The art/science of analyzing written communication for the purpose of personality evaluation.

**Handwriting-improvement program.** A system that introduces the idea of movement, space, and form through form-drawing exercises for the purpose of achieving clear, legible handwriting.

**Handwriting sample.** Any writing offered to a graphologist for the purpose of analysis.

**Hieroglyphics.** Pictorial writing created by the early Egyptians. Now sometimes used as a derisive description of poor handwriting.

**Hook.** An involuntary curved or angular formation in the handwriting, often found as an initial or terminal stroke.

**Ideograms.** Pictures used as symbols for ideas.

**Illegible writing.** Deteriorated writing caused by speed or faulty execution. Any part of a letter or word taken out of context that cannot be deciphered is illegible.

**Inflated loops.** Loops in handwriting expanded to a size larger than that prescribed by standard copybook form.

**Lead-in stroke.** See *Beginning stroke.*

**Learning disability.** A neurological or physiological blockage that impairs the ability to learn in a normal teaching environment.

**Left brain.** The left half of the cerebrum. The hemisphere of the brain believed to control verbal and analytical functions.

**Left-handedness.** Use of the left hand as the dominant hand, with the right hand playing the secondary role.

**Legibility.** A quality of handwriting that is clear in arrangement and detail. Writing that is readable and clear even when parts are taken out of context.

**Letter.** A standardized character used in writing or printing to represent a speech sound. There are twenty-six letters in the English alphabet.

**Linear.** A quality of handwriting that appears lean and tall. Linear handwriting is characterized by narrow ovals and/or loops, angular formations, and general simplification.

**Loop.** A writing formation in Upper Zone and Lower Zone letters in which space is enclosed between upstrokes and downstrokes.

**Lower Zone.** The writing area that embodies the part of each letter that descends below the Middle Zone. There are six bizonal letters that begin at the baseline and descend into the Lower Zone: *g, j, p, q, y,* and *z.*

**Lower Zone elaboration.** Embellished Lower Zone formations. Includes extra strokage, curlicues, or expansion, both horizontal and vertical.

**Lower Zone length.** The distance from the baseline to the lowest point in the Lower Zone to which the loop or stroke extends.

**Majuscule alphabet.** The capital letter forms introduced by the Romans and later enhanced by the Irish in the Book of Kells.

**Margins.** The top, bottom, and side spaces on the page. They frame the body of written, typed, or printed matter.

**Middle Zone.** The writing area that embodies part or all of every letter of the alphabet. Letters occupying only the Middle Zone are *a, c, e, i, m, n, o, r, s, u, v, w,* and *x.* The Middle Zone is the area of handwriting from the baseline to the top of these letters.

**Minuscule alphabet.** The lower-case letter forms introduced by the Romans and later enhanced by the Irish in the Book of Kells.

**Mirror drawing.** The production of a form drawing on one side of a line that directly models the form on the opposite side of the line.

**Mirror writing.** Writing that begins at the right and moves left. Letters are reversed, so the writing can be read easily only by looking in a mirror.

**Movement.** How the handwriting moves across the paper. Movement encompasses the speed and pressure of writing as well as expansion, direction, and rhythm.

**Organization.** The qualities of balance, rhythm, and harmony found in a writing sample. Includes harmonious arrangement of margins, letter form, and word and line space.

**Palmer method.** A system of writing developed by A. N. Palmer that advocated a rapid, plain, and muscular movement. The method stressed arm movement and made use of exercises performed with rolling movements of the arm from the shoulder to the wrist. The fingers were to remain passive.

**Papyrus.** A writing material made from the papyrus plant and used by early Egyptians, Romans, and Greeks.

**Phonogram.** A symbol that represents a sound.

**Pictogram.** A stylized symbol of an object.

**Picture value.** The arrangement, form, and movement of writing that contains enough originality, rhythm, and form level to provide a pleasing picture.

**Preconscious.** Pertaining to that part of a person's mental activity that is not immediately conscious but can be easily recalled.

**Pressure.** The third dimension of writing. The energy applied to the writing instrument, causing it to produce an impression on the paper and to create embossing on the back of the paper.

**Primary pressure.** Pen pressure on the writing surface exerted by shoulder, upper arm, forearm, and hand—not by the fingers.

**Printing.** A form of written communication consisting of individual letter forms not joined by any connectives.

**Rebus device.** The combination of two or more phonograms to make up a word.

**Release.** Freedom of movement in the writing, as opposed to contraction.

**Retrace.** Concealed stroke. One stroke hides a previously executed stroke.

**Rhythm.** A complex feature of handwriting reflecting the natural heartbeat and pulse within the writing. Graphologically found in the balance and symmetry of the writing pattern. Harmony in arrangement, form, and movement presents a rhythmic picture value.

**Right brain.** The right half of the cerebrum. The hemisphere of the brain believed to control nonverbal and global functions.

**Scribble.** Playful self-expression with a writing instrument. Aimless marking on a paper. Patterns practiced in childhood may persist into adulthood, where they are revealed in doodles.

**Secondary pressure.** The force on the writing instrument applied by the fingers.

**Sensory/motor integration.** A balancing of the input to the senses with the motor output of their impression.

**Shading.** Contrasting pressure between thin upstrokes and thick downstrokes or vice versa.

**Signature.** Name or symbol used on a legal or personal document to identify the signer. A signature may consist of one or more names depending on the custom of the writer's country. As a rule, a signer has both a formal and an informal signature.

**Signature congruence.** A measure of similarity between the signature and the body of the writing.

**Simplicity.** A quality in writing that sheds nonessential strokes from letters, including beginning and ending strokes, to facilitate speed and clarity.

**Size of writing.** A relative term, based on the size of the Middle Zone. Standard copybook Middle Zone height is three millimeters. Upper and Lower Zone extensions should be made in proportion to Middle Zone height.

**Slant.** The leftward or rightward direction of the writing as it moves away from the baseline.

**Slow writing.** Carefully executed writing—usually rounded, large, and monotonous.

**Spacing.** The arrangement of the writing on the page. The relative placement of margins, letters, words, and lines.

**Speed.** Tempo of writing movement. Speed depends on many things, including writing position, the writer's comfort, the time available for writing, and the reason for the written communication. Speed is affected by the writer's nervous temperament and his or her training and practice with the writing instrument.

**Spencerian script.** A style of writing popular in the early nineteenth century. Right-slanted, semiangular writing noted for its beauty and shading.

**Stroke.** A single writing movement that begins with a dot and continues until direction is changed. A stroke may be long or short, curved or straight, thick or thin, blunt or pointed. There are six basic strokes: dot, line, curve, hook, circle, and loop.

**Style.** Any distinctive form and movement in handwriting. Some basic writing styles are cursive, printing, artistic, copybook, simplified, and elaborated.

**Symbol.** A letter, figure, mark, or combination of these used to designate a specific idea. That which represents something else.

**Tension.** Contraction within the handwriting; restraint. Tension is revealed in the handwriting by cramped letters, retracings, narrowness, and close spacing.

**Tension/release.** Variations in writing pressure that correspond to the muscular tension and release occurring during the writing process.

**Thread.** One of the four basic connective forms in handwriting. An indistinct connective that tapers to a sinuous, wavy, or threadlike stroke.

**Tic.** A short, involuntary, inflexible stroke at the beginning of a word or letter. Sometimes called a "temper tic."

**Trigger thumb.** A syndrome that exists when a bump in the flexor tendon causes the tendon to get hung up on the tight-pulley flexor, resulting in a triggering of the thumb.

**Trizonal.** A writing movement that encompasses all three zones. The letter *f* is the only natural trizonal letter. However, many writers make capitals that dip into the Lower Zone unnaturally or reach into the Upper Zone without cause.

**Underscore.** The line under a signature or any other part of the writing to emphasize its meaning.

**Upper Zone.** The writing area that embodies the part of each letter that reaches above the Middle Zone. There are six bizonal letters that begin at the baseline and reach into the Upper Zone: *b, d, h, k, l,* and *t*.

**Upstroke.** Any part of a letter that proceeds in an upward direction.

**Word space.** The distance between words. The width of the normal word space is equal to the height of the Middle Zone.

**Zaner-Bloser.** A style of writing commonly used in American schools; a spin-off of the Palmer method.

**Zones.** The division of writing into three areas, the Middle, Upper, and Lower Zones. It was developed by Max Pulver, a Swiss graphologist.

# Bibliography

Allport, G. W., and Vernon, P. E. *Studies in Expressive Movement.* New York: Macmillan, 1933, 1967.

Armstrong, Thomas. *In Their Own Way.* Los Angeles: Jeremy P. Tarcher, 1987.

Brookes, Mona. *Drawing with Children.* Los Angeles: Jeremy P. Tarcher, 1986.

Edwards, Betty. *Drawing on the Right Side of the Brain.* Los Angeles: Jeremy P. Tarcher, 1979.

Gladich, J., and Sassi, P. *The Write Approach, Books I and II.* San Diego: Handwriting Consultants International, 1988.

Griffin, J. R., and Walton, H. N. *Dyslexia Determination Test (DDT) Kit.* Los Angeles: I-MED Instructional Materials and Equipment Distributors, 1981.

Hamilton, Charles. *Book of Autographs.* New York: Book Creations, Inc., 1978.

Inlander, Charles B., Levin, Lowell S., and Weiner, Ed. *Medicine on Trial.* New York: Prentice-Hall Press, 1988.

Jackson, Donald. *The Story of Writing.* London: Taplinger Publishing Company, 1981.

Kraut, Leila. *Handwriting Exercises and Dyslexia.* Translated by Erika Margarete Karohs. Pebble Beach, Calif.: Erika Margarete Karohs, 1983.

McAllen, Audrey E. *The Extra Lesson—Exercises in Movement, Drawing and Painting for Helping Children in Difficulties with Writing, Reading and Arithmetic.* Gloucester, England: Robinswood Press, 1980. (Rudolf Steiner College, 9200 Fair Oaks Blvd., Fair Oaks, Calif.)

————. *Teaching Children to Write.* London: Rudolf Steiner Press, 1977.

Niederhauser, H. R., and Frohlich, M. *Form Drawing.* Spring Valley, N.Y.: Mercury Press, 1984.

Orton, Samuel T. *Reading, Writing and Speech Problems in Children.* New York: W. W. Norton and Company, 1964.

Oussoren, Ragnhild. *Writing-Movement-Therapy.* San Diego: Handwriting Consultants International, 1986.

PeBenito, Rhandy. "Developmental Gerstmann Syndrome: Case Report and Review of the Literature." *Developmental and Behavioral Pediatrics* 8, no. 4 (1987): 229–232.

Richards, John H. *The Gerstmann Syndrome, Problems with Space and Ordering.* San Diego: Kaiser Permanente Center for School Problems, 1982.

Roman, Klara. *Encyclopedia of the Written Word.* New York: Fredrick Ungar Publishing, 1968.

————. *Handwriting, A Key to Personality.* New York: Pantheon Books, 1952.

Sassi, P. A., and Whiting, E. *Personal Worth Course.* San Diego: Handwriting Consultants International, 1983.

Saudek, Robert. *Experiments with Handwriting.* Sacramento: Books for Professionals, 1978.

Whiting, Eldene, ed. *Glossary of Standard Terms Used in Handwriting Analysis.* San Diego: Handwriting Consultants International, 1983.

Whiting, Eldene. *Traitmatch.* San Diego: Handwriting Consultants International, 1988.

Wolff, Werner. *Diagrams of the Unconscious.* New York: Grune and Stratton, 1965.

Wonder, J., and Donovan, P. *Whole-Brain Thinking.* New York: William Morrow and Company, 1984.

For more information on the 30-day Handwriting Improvement Program, handwriting analysis, courses, and related publications, contact:

**Handwriting Consultants International**
9974 Scripps Ranch Blvd., Box 318
San Diego, CA 92131
619/586-1511